A
CHARISMATIC
APPROACH
TO
SOCIAL
ACTION

Larry Christenson

A CHARISMATIC APPROACH TO SOCIAL ACTION

bethany fellowship

MINNEAPOLIS, MINNESOTA

Library of Congress Cataloging in Publication Data

Christenson, Laurence.
A Charismatic Approach to Social Action.
1. Pentecostalism.
2. Church and social problems.
I. Title.
BX8763.C48
261.8'3
74-1326
ISBN 0-87123-389-4

Published by Bethany Fellowship, Inc.
6820 Auto Club Road
Minneapolis, Minnesota 55438

Printed in the United States of America

INTRODUCTION

The book of *Judges* tells the story of a band of Gilead-ites who stood guard at the fords of the Jordan River. They forced everyone who tried to cross over to say the word "shibboleth." If the person pronounced it "sibboleth," he was detected as coming from the wrong part of the country, and was not allowed to cross over. From this incident, the word *shibboleth* has passed into the idiom of our language, as a test or watchword.

To a considerable degree, "social action" has become a shibboleth in the religious culture of our day. It is a test question that is put to every ministry or religious movement. "What are you doing about the problems of society?"

The reader of this book, who has his ear tuned for traditional social action sounds, will detect certain unaccustomed intonations. But traditional evangelicals will also detect unfamiliar accents.

A shibboleth is not enough. The whole question of social action has become stalemated with slogans and cliches. A more exhaustive interrogation is needed. There needs to be an examination of some of the underlying *principles* relating to Christian social action.

In 1971-72, I was invited to spend a year's sabbatical study at The Institute for Ecumenical and Cultural Research, Collegeville, Minnesota. It was there that the initial work on this book was undertaken. In my study of the charismatic movement, I saw the beginning of what I believe to be a new breakthrough in the field of Christian social action. This book is an attempt to share some of the observations and considerations which have come out of this study.

Much of what is happening in the charismatic movement of social significance is still in embryo form, just beginning to show itself. The movement is far from being a paradigm of effective social action. The ideas expressed here are as much a call to action for the charismatic movement, as they are a description of certain things that are beginning to happen.

Yet one quality which undisputably is present in the charismatic movement is *vitality*. It is my prayer that this vitality will more and more express itself along lines of redemptive, healing, and truly biblical social action.

My thanks are especially due to Dr. Kilian McDonnell, O.S.B., director of the Institute, for the invitation and encouragement to do this study.

All Saints Day, 1973   Larry Christenson

TABLE OF CONTENTS

Chapter One
WHAT IS THE CHURCH DOING?

We live in a day when critics inside and outside the church have raised the cry for Christian social action. "What is the church doing about injustice, war, poverty, racism, ecology?" The question is rhetorical, not really a question at all. It is a critique: "The church is not doing enough, if indeed it is doing anything at all!"

What answer shall be given to the critics, who scold the church because she does not plunge into some of the churning social issues of our day? It is not enough to answer rhetoric with rhetoric: "What business does the church have getting mixed up in worldly affairs?" The demand for social action deserves from the church a carefully thought-out response. For if we stay with it long enough to get past the rhetoric, we find that the cry for social action challenges us to think through, and define afresh, for our age, the purpose and mission of the church in the world.

One answer to the cry for social action, which has begun to emerge in recent years, is something we might call "a charismatic approach to social action."

"Charismatic" is a transliterated term, from the Greek *charisma*. The root meaning is, "a gift or favor freely and graciously given."[1] In the New Testament it is especially used to designate special gifts of a non-material sort, bestowed by the grace of God on individual Christians.

Since the early 1960's, the word has been used to characterize a widespread renewal movement in the historic churches. An important feature of the movement has been the experience of gifts or *charismata* of the Holy Spirit, especially those mentioned by St. Paul in I Corinthians 12:8-11: the word of wisdom, the word of knowledge, faith, healing, miracles, prophecy, discernment of spirits, speaking in tongues, and the interpretation of tongues. The term, however, has come to have a general application, referring simply to the movement itself. Our use of the term "charismatic" is primarily in this historical sense, and only secondarily in a theological sense. By common usage this historical phenomenon has come to be known as "the charismatic movement." It designates something which, though diverse and variegated, is nevertheless historically identifiable. When we speak of "charismatic approach," we mean the kind of approach that one encounters within the broad context of this particular renewal movement.

This does not mean that we divorce the word from its theological context. The theological focus or emphasis which one finds in the charismatic movement certainly warrants the use of "charismatic" in a general sense. The central feature of the charismatic movement, as Roman Catholic scholar Kilian McDonnell has pointed out, is not merely the gifts, but "fulness of life in the Holy Spirit."[2] The potentiality of the gifts of the Holy Spirit is a matter of constant reckoning in the charismatic movement. In every situation one is open to the supernatural working of God. It is, as Henry P. Van Dusen has said in characterizing the Pentecostal phenomenon generally, the awareness of "God present, and God active."[3]

A "charismatic" approach to social issues may thus awaken or call into manifestation gifts of the Holy Spirit in specific situations. But the focus of attention is not upon the gifts, as such. It is, rather, this broader issue of the Holy Spirit's direct involvement in the issues which are approached. *A charismatic approach to social issues is one which is both initiated and carried out in the power of the Holy Spirit* — not merely as a theological principle, but as an experienced event. It is distinguished from a rationalistic or pragmatic or so-called common sense approach, which simply reasons from a general principle to a practical application, with little or no sense of God's active participation in the process. A charismatic approach to social issues cannot conclude its inquiry merely by asking, "Is this thing necessary? Is it good?" The prior question must be faced. "Does the *Lord* initiate this? Is *His* Spirit the motivating Spirit? Can we confidently expect His supernatural power and resources in this undertaking?"

At a church convention in Los Angeles, shortly after the Watts' riots in 1965, it was reported that several white couples in the San Fernando Valley had sold their homes, and were moving with their families down to Watts, to share the life and the problems of the people there. This was received with amazement, but with the obvious approval of the delegates. Then a lay leader from one of the congregations spoke up: "If the Lord has sent them down to Watts, more power to them. They will be blessed, and they will be a blessing. God finishes what He begins. But if they are going down there on the basis of their own sympathy or enthusiasm, I can only pity them and their children."[4]

This, one might say, would be the charismatic point. *A specific sense of call and direction by the Holy Spirit is at the heart of a charismatic approach to social issues.* Lacking that, any action by the church, no matter how well-intentioned, will lead ultimately to frustration and disillusionment. "Unless the Lord builds the house, those who build it labor in vain."[5.]

Jim Cavnar, one of the coordinators of "The Word of God," a charismatic Christian community in Ann Arbor, Michigan, told of the pressure they experienced to "get involved" in social issues, in the early stages of their community life.

"We had to resist that pressure from the outside," he said, "because God was saying something else to us. Our first call was to 'build a community.' And now, some years later, we see the wisdom of God's plan. By putting our emphasis on building a Christian community, we have been more successful in serving the larger community than if we had plunged at once into a lot of 'projects.' "[6.]

The first wave of the charismatic movement might be compared to a new surge of life which came to a man who has been lying semiconscious in a hospital. You don't at once dash in and roust him out of bed for a day of hard physical labor. First he must gain strength; he must resume the normal functions which sustain and strengthen life.

During the first few years of the charismatic movement, the emphasis was very much on prayer, Bible study, and the spiritual growth of the individual. This initial emphasis on personal spiritual awakening was a necessary first step. For many in the church, spiritual life was at a low ebb. People who may have been considerably involved in religious activity discovered within themselves a spiritual dryness and hunger. The charismatic renewal came as a fresh pulsation of spiritual life.

Interest in "activity" and "programs" gave way to an

experiential re-discovery of the reality of the Christian faith. Caught up in this movement of the Spirit, people began to re-learn the ways of faith and of prayer. "Looked at from the outside," said a leading Catholic researcher of the movement, "it could almost be mistaken for a prayer movement."[7] But inside, other forces were also at work.

The initial emphasis on personal spiritual awakening indicated that the charismatic movement has a clear-cut affinity for evangelical theology. Some aspects of the movement, such as the "Jesus People," have even been dubbed a revival of fundamentalist Christianity (with a touch of frontier revivalism).

Any genuine move of the Spirit surely will underscore basic truths of the faith, as part of its total proclamation. It can be helpful to note similarities between the charismatic renewal and other movements in the church, either past or present.* But we do not understand or explain a fresh movement of the Spirit simply by pasting a familiar label on it. We must look beyond the similarities. We must also discover that which is different.

Evangelical theology, with its emphasis on personal salvation, has sometimes neglected issues which arise out of man's social or corporate existence. The theology of social action has in some ways been a reaction against a one-sided emphasis on the individual. But, as is frequently the case when one reacts against something, social activism has often ended up adopting some of the more negative features of a one-sided evangelicalism — rigid dogmatism, legalistic standards of behavior, self-righteousness.

While the charismatic movement has underscored the

---

*In this regard, see the author's book, *A Message to the Charismatic Movement*, which draws lessons for the present-day movement from the experience of the Catholic Apostolic Church in England, in the 19th Century.

central importance of the personal in Christianity, it has more lately also been moved by a concern for the social. At an interdenominational conference of charismatic leaders, Ralph Wilkerson, pastor of one of the largest charismatic churches in the country, said, "I want to show the world the 'youth concern' and the 'social concern' of the charismatic movement."[8] This kind of emphasis does not appear to come as a reaction against the earlier emphasis on personal awakening and growth, for that continues undiminished. It is, rather, an awareness that the purposes of the Spirit extend beyond the individual, his relationship with God, and his personal piety.

The focus of social concern in the charismatic movement, however, does not leap directly from the individual to the problems of society. A critical intermediate step intervenes, which gives a distinctive form and style to the social action which is emerging in the charismatic movement. This is the emphasis on "community."

The social action which results is more than: a) a tabulation of charitable deeds done by so many separate individual Christians (the individualistic approach), b) a loosely knit coalition of Christian groups and individuals who join forces to help effect certain changes in the political or social arena (the social activist approach). Rather, the social action is an outgrowth of the community. The primary commitment is not to a "cause," but to a community. People are drawn together to share not only their faith or their resolve, but their lives.

Various kinds of communities are emerging, from a cluster of extended households to full communal fellowships. And from these communities flows forth a demonstration of Christ's love, in a variety of practical works. In one city, a whole household receives and acts upon prophetic revelation to move into the ghetto, and become there a center of friendship, service, and witness. In another locality, numerous households literally push out their walls to take in orphans. A legal-aid clinic is set up to help people in one poverty area. Drug addicts, dropouts, deserted mothers, or lonely widows find themselves drawn in among people, where life-in-community is opening up new possibilities for translating the love of Christ into action.

Beneath an almost bewildering variety of social works, one discovers a common thread: *A conscious sense of the Spirit's initiative.* Communities of Christians are being formed, and are entering into particular social works, in the context of a movement which lays special emphasis upon prayer, prophecy, revelation. As important as the work itself, is the conviction that this is a work which the Holy Spirit specifically sets before this community.

From this conviction springs another: that which the Holy Spirit has initiated, He will also support. The work is carried out with a conscious dependence upon His active working, not excluding the miraculous. It is this expectation of the Holy Spirit's active involvement which pervades the works of social action emerging in the charismatic movement.

Chapter Two
THE FAILURE OF PHARISAISM

The early Christian Church faced the problem of Pharisaism, the tendency to translate the Gospel into a new Law. "O foolish Galatians," wrote the apostle Paul, "Who has bewitched you? Having begun with the Spirit, are you now ending with the flesh?"[9.]

Pharisaism is more than the attempt to reduce Christianity to a system of rules and regulations. That is only its obvious outward characteristic. The essence of Pharisaism is a *mentality*. It looks upon religion as a responsibility, something that must be *done*. God is the Lawgiver and Judge, who lays down the rules; that is His part in the whole enterprise. Man's part is to win God's approval by keeping the rules.

Pharisaism has little sense of God's active involvement in man's religious experience; other, perhaps, than to visit punishments on those who don't keep the rules, in the form of accidents, misfortune, and sickness. God draws up the blueprint, but it is up to man to build the edifice of his religion. The flexibility, the sense of give-and-take which characterizes a personal relationship, is foreign to the spirit of Pharisaism. The focus of one's expectations is centered on man. It is a stance of self-sufficiency. Its favorite text is, "God helps those who help themselves."

Every religious movement must guard itself against the danger of Pharisaism. It slips in unannounced. It mingles among people who have experienced an outpouring of spiritual life. It bandies about religious terminology with glib facility. Its zeal and earnestness gain attention and commendation. It fastens upon the readiness for dedication in the newly awakened. Its objectives are so praiseworthy, and its goals so unimpeachable, that the exhortations can scarcely be gainsaid. "You want to be *truly* holy, don't you? If you are *really* a Christian, surely you will join in supporting this...." Subtly the focus shifts from what God does to what man must do. Those who began as witnesses to a work of God, turn and become lawgivers to one another.

This is one of the great challenges which faces the present day charismatic movement. Will it be able to ward off the encroachment of Pharisaism? The problem is not theoretical. One already turns up evidences of it in charismatic prayer groups and communities. The flavor may be evangelical, or it may be social activist, but the mentality is essentially the same: "Now that you are back down to earth, let's get to work and *do*..." — in which the "doing" is a call to human effort and achievement.

Lennox Palin, a Baptist minister, speaking before a ministerial fellowship in San Pedro, California in 1968, pointed up an interesting but little-noted fact: While the "evangelical" and the "social activist" espouse different causes, they operate with the same essential *mentality*. In both, there is a tendency to operate within a theological "box," a closed system of ready-made answers, with little understanding or regard for other points-of-view. The evangelical has his set of texts, centering on the personal experience of salvation, and a life of holiness. The social activist has his, emphasizing man's social responsibility. There is little real acquaintance with pertinent literature in the other's field. Outside one's own box, discussion tends to be in the nature of an exchange of pejorative slogans and cliches. The intellectual disdain of the activist for the evangelical's "fundamentalism" is matched by the evangelical's contempt for a "watered-down gospel of secular humanism."

Pharisaism thrives in this kind of an environment. Entrenched in a narrow position, a group tends to become defensive. Theological expression becomes more rigid and dogmatic. "Right belief" loses the characteristic of a joyful expression of faith, and becomes more and more a self-righteous polemic. The faith is not something we have humbly received, but something we self-confidently *do*.

Hand in hand with "right belief" goes a standard of "right action." As Pharisaism infiltrates one's theology, it will inevitably determine the character of his ethics. A narrowly self-confident theology gives rise to a narrow, self-righteous ethic.

Jesus' critique of the Pharisees was essentially twofold: 1) Their concerns, which may have been right and good in themselves, were too narrowly conceived; the problem was not so much with what they did, as with what they left undone. 2) Their attitude toward others was severely judgmental; anyone whose beliefs or actions deviated from their established norms fell under their condemnation. Such attitudes result in pride, hostility, division.

When such attitudes prevail, one can predict a widespread failure of the church to make a convincing and wholesome impact upon society. And this in fact is what has happened. Much of the church's effort in the social arena has ended in fragmentation, frustration, and disillusionment. The evangelical may blame this on the social activist's secularization of the Gospel, and the activist may charge it to the evangelical's lack of social concern. But this touches only the surface of the problem.

If we assign the failure to the evangelical or to the social activist we miss the point. The failure is the failure of Pharisaism — the spirit that says, "This is what you must do in order to be a first-class Christian." A legalistic spirit, by its very nature, evokes a negative or hostile response. The impasse between evangelicals and social activists is rooted in the spirit of Pharisaism which has made inroads into both camps.

Over the years, evangelical movements have grown accustomed to the charge of narrow exclusivism. The same characteristic, however, is also present in the social action movement, though this fact is seldom noted. It is important that we recognize this, for it helps us to understand why the church's response to social needs has tended to become rigid and inflexible.

Today's architects of social concern have focused attention on too narrow a spectrum of human problems and needs. Like the pious legalists of a former day, they have drawn up an approved list of Do's and Don't's.

Back then it was things like, "Don't smoke, don't drink, don't dance, don't play cards; do go to church, do belong to the Ladies' Aid, do say your prayers, do demand respect from your children, do contribute to the Mission Box — these are the things that add up to holiness." Any or all of these things might be good and helpful in one's personal Christian life, but holiness can neither be circumscribed nor arrived at by so narrow a listing.

Today the scene has shifted from the personal to the social arena, but the mentality is essentially the same: Don't discriminate, don't support war, don't buy table grapes; do fight poverty, do fight pollution, do support the

UN — these are stands which qualify you as a genuinely concerned Christian." Again, any or all of these things might be considered issues worthy of a Christian's support. But Christian compassion cannot be crammed into a narrow legalistic straightjacket.

One could mention, almost at random, a dozen or more issues, equally urgent in our society, which for some reason one rarely encounters in the typical listing of social issues —

• The decline of our free institutions (educational, charitable), and its consequence to the future of a free society.

• Our inefficient, confused, and inequitable system of taxation.

• The coercive, monopolistic power of giant labor unions.

• The increasing tolerance of lawless behavior in our society.

• Irresponsible fiscal policy at the governmental level, and its demoralizing effects upon personal integrity.

• Increasing disregard for authority in all sectors.

• Blatant contempt for personal rights (the inevitable harbinger of tyranny), both by agencies of government, and by self-appointed revolutionaries.

• Our increasingly confused and confusing system of justice, whereby interminable delays, hair-splitting technicalities, and sky-rocketing costs conspire to thwart the swift and fair judgment of a case.

• The increasing tendency, in the name of "rights" and "justice," to regard people as members of rigidly defined groups, rather than as individuals.

• The disintegration of family life, and its deleterious effects upon the society as a whole.

• The plight of the elderly, who come to retirement and find their lifetime savings eroded away by inflation.

- The increasing tendency of our government to intervene in the private lives of its citizens, with the dread potential for tyranny.

- The failure of the American government to render justice to Japanese-Americans for the property which was virtually expropriated from them during World War II.

- The sorry state of elementary and secondary education among us, which on the one hand clamors for constantly improved physical facilities and equipment, and on the other hand contents itself with shoddier and shoddier levels of student performance.

The above is a purely random listing of general issues. It does not even touch on the countless local needs which exist within walking distance of any Christian congregation. What should Christians do about the widows in their own congregations, who grow into old age alone, and anxious about who will care for them, when they can no longer care for themselves? What about the dope traffic at our local junior high school? And the beautiful parks in our town – that are no longer safe for our children, because they have become the haunt of rowdies and perverts?

The point is this: *The spectrum of social needs is much broader and much more diverse than the usual listing of issues which receives publicity in the religious media.* The reason for this is evident, but it is often overlooked. In the very nature of the case, we must be *selective* when we address ourselves to social issues.

Every morning when you wake up, a thousand human needs beckon within walking distance of your own home; millions more beyond your immediate neighborhood, throughout the nation and the world. Even if you spent full time at it, you could address yourself to but a fraction of these human needs and issues. No matter how great your concern, you would, of necessity, have to choose some certain needs with which you would involve yourself, while letting others go.

This much is self-evident. No one person or group can respond to the full spectrum of needs and causes which clamor for attention in the social arena. But right here is where discussion and thinking about social issues often get bogged down. The "social activist," who wants the Church to do something about human needs, is pitted against the "evangelical," who wants the Church to stick to the business of preaching the Gospel. Closer examination reveals this to be a false and abstract dichotomy. The non-activist evangelical is a straw man, existing only in theory and rhetoric. This is not to say that there are not Christians whose concern for the preaching of the Gospel is absolutely primary. But this primary concern does not deactivate them from social involvement. It merely indicates the primary line along which their activity chooses to express itself. Their point of difference with the social activist is not involvement versus non-involvement, but rather this business of selection. Faced with the inevitable necessity of choosing which needs one will respond to, the social activist and the evangelical have drawn up different sets of priorities.

It is especially important to recognize this in the case of the evangelical. For even the most avowed evangelical does not spend twenty-four hours a day preaching the Gospel. His time is given to a whole host of activities. And, upon closer examination, one usually finds that most evangelicals have not a few social concerns – things they would like to see changed or bettered in the society around them, causes which they are quite prepared to become involved in personally.

An evangelical one time set up a luncheon meeting. On

several occasions he had fulminated against the social activists. The "social gospel," he felt, was a blunting, even an outright betrayal, of the Christian faith. "The church has no business getting mixed up in politics and social issues." Yet this luncheon meeting was called for the purpose of initiating a petition to the City Council, to tighten up enforcement of anti-pornography legislation. At this point, by any reasonable standard of judgment, the "evangelical" was behaving like a "social activist."

We do not at all need to criticize the evangelical's concern for the primacy of the preaching of the Gospel. That is a valid concern. Nor do we need to undermine his case against some of the activities which are being promoted under the banner of Christianity today, in the name of social concern; his critique merits patient scrutiny. But our reasoning with one another needs to become more accurate and precise. The essential difference between activists and evangelicals is not over *whether* we should become involved in society, but over *where* and *how* we should become involved. The simple truth of the matter is, *all* of us are "social activists," properly understood.

Phillip Berrigan burned draft files because he was against the war in Vietnam. Carl McIntyre headed up a victory march in Washington to muster support for the same war. To say that one is a revolutionary, or the other a reactionary, simply describes the kind of social action toward which each one inclines. The revolutionary has drawn up his list of concerns, the reactionary his; and liberals, moderates, and conservatives theirs.

At a national church convention, a whole list of "crisis issues" crowded the agenda: hunger, racism, urban blight, conscientious objection. In the midst of it all, a man stood up and said, "When are we going to say a word on behalf of the chickens and the cows?" Stunned silence, then a tittering here and there. The man went on, passionately serious: "What kind of stewardship and care of God's creatures is it, when we coop up thousands and thousands of chickens in little cages so small they can't even turn around, never let them out to scratch around in the barn-yard, just force-feed them to get higher and higher egg production, with never a thought about them as individual creatures made by God with maybe some feelings of their own? Or the cows. Crowd them into a black-topped corral, just so you can hose away the manure more easily, never letting them out into a good green pasture to eat some grass and lie in the shade for a while; just feed them a bunch of concentrate to up your beef production, and don't let the bulls and cows get together, just call in your artificial insemination man once a year and turn him loose with that big syringe. I ask you, is that the way God wants us to treat His creatures?"[10.] The convention, scarcely suppressing a chuckle, thanked him politely for his comments, and went back to a consideration of the "social issues."

This little incident provided a bit of comic relief, in the midst of what often becomes too-sober ecclesiastical deliberations anyway. But it points up the inaccurate and stereotyped labels which confuse much of our discussion about social issues. The man who spoke up for the chickens and the cows got no more than an amused hearing—not because the social activists, as such, were dominating the convention, for this man was a social activist too. His misfortune came from the fact that the item on his list did not happen to be on anyone else's list.

We all have our lists. It cannot be otherwise. No one person or group can be actively concerned about everything. In the nature of the case, we must be selective about our involvement in social issues, choosing some, letting others go.

We do not fault the social activist because he has drawn

up a list of concerns. *What we call into question is a self-righteous Pharisaism which draws up a narrow list of issues and says, "This is THE list of valid social issues."* Any serious reading of our society must turn up dozens of situations which should be rectified, but which for some reason seldom rate mention in the religious media, or at the level of official church pronouncements. Why is it that the great majority of those who purport to speak for the church (denominational officials, editorialists, theologians) have confined their expressions of social concern to a relatively narrow spectrum of issues? Why have they bypassed dozens of issues on their way to publicizing a few? And what might this portend for the church, and her mission in the world? To answer these questions, we must take note of certain moods in the secular culture, and their influence upon Christian social theory.

Chapter Three

THE INFLUENCE OF THE STATUS QUO

By its very nature, social action tends toward correction. It addresses itself to things being done which ought not be done, or things not being done which ought to be done. And this, in turn, can spell unpopularity, even persecution, for those who propose the corrective. Ingrained and comfortable habits do not change happily, nor do revolutionary passions yield readily to admonition. Human nature rebels against being corrected.

Knowing this to be true, the Christian stands in particular danger: Instead of patiently seeking the mind of the Lord as one draws up his list of social concerns, he can all too easily become intimidated by the climate of opinion which prevails in his particular sector of society. Instead of making a distinctive witness as a Christian, he ends up as a mere echo of the status quo.

The status quo, of course, is simply the power or custom or authority which prevails in a particular culture at a particular time.

The church has often been portrayed, even caricatured, as a bastion of the status quo. Most often this falls as an epithet upon the evangelical. He is pictured as upholding the social, political, and economic doctrines of the 19th Century with the same ferocious zeal that he upholds a conservative biblical theology.

There is some truth in this, but in order to be understood, it must be seen in the right context. Evangelicalism does not in itself harbor an innate resistance to social change. Historically, evangelicals have exerted a profound influence upon society.

"Evangelicalism," says Ian Bradley, young Oxford historian, "was the most powerful religious movement in the late eighteenth century." He goes on to tell how the Evangelicals literally reshaped the social and political structures of England in the nineteenth century. "The 'Saints,' as they were nicknamed by their contemporaries, felt called to fight sin wherever they found it. The gradual winning round of public opinion had much to do with the Saints' most spectacular success, the abolition of the British slave trade in 1807. Perhaps the most purely altruistic measure ever passed in Parliament, it was the result of a twenty-five year campaign under the direction of William Wilberforce, the slightly built, vivacious Yorkshire MP who was the leader of the Evangelicals in Parliament....

"The Saints raised the tone of politics and society out of all recognition. The Commons had been manifestly interested only in itself; politics was a corrupt business of borough-mongering and place-seeking; the aristocracy were decadent and debauched. The Evangelical Revival changed all this: Parliament stopped debating game laws and enclosures and began to discuss prison reform and the rights and wrongs of colonial slavery. Politics became an exercise in morality; the aristocracy assumed a high seriousness and devoted themselves to good works. Above all, a middle class that might so easily have lost faith in the prevailing political system found satisfaction in taking up great moral causes.

"The best in Evangelicalism was what came out in the bitter struggle against vested interest and cynicism. Here it emerged as a radical, dynamic creed compatible only with the keenest intellectual rigor and the most careful conscience-searching."[11.]

Not only in politics, but also in Christian circles, the evangelical awakenings gave rise to works of social concern. While the 'Saints' were establishing child labor laws and prison reforms, Christian groups like the YMCA were springing up, and William Booth's Salvation Army was reaching out to the "lowest and the worst" in the slums of London.

The evangelical moved confidently in the social milieu of the 19th Century, because, for him, the theological center-of-gravity was in the right place. The concern for social reform never displaced a primary emphasis upon the need for personal salvation. If we trace it out historically, the evangelical's identification with the 19th Century is at root an identification with a *theological* status quo.

In the late 19th, and early 20th Centuries, this theological position came under attack from various quarters.

The school of "higher criticism" coming out of Germany seemed to undermine the authority and reliability of the Bible.

Darwinism seemed to offer an explanation of the world and of creation which, if it did not make God unnecessary, at least edged Him off center stage. While its ostensible field of inquiry was biological evolution, evangelicals rightly intuited that imbedded in the theories of Darwin were significant theological implications. Garret Vanderkooi, assistant professor at the Institute for Enzyme Research at the University of Wisconsin, has pointed out that the weakness of the evolutionary hypothesis is being increasingly recognized by members of the scientific community, especially in light of research in the field of biochemistry. "A theory of such vast scope," he contends, "would undoubtedly be passed off as idle speculation, *if it were not for its theological implications*...it offers a naturalistic account of creation...for those who do not want to recognize the Creator."[12.]

When Karl Marx leveled his critique against capitalism, he let part of his ire fall on religion, and Christianity in particular, as the "opiate of the people."

The "social Gospel," popularized by Walter Rauschenbusch, seemed to shunt aside a concern for personal salvation, in favor of social reform.

Faced with these onslaughts, the evangelical mounted his defenses. Though his initial concern was to protect the vital center of individual salvation, little by little the perimeters of defense were extended. He took up common cause with those who hoisted the banner of individualism, against the collectivist mindset which was slowly pervading Western culture. Along with the issue of individual salvation, he found himself locked in a defense of individualism across a wide spectrum of the secular scene.

The tenets of a free enterprise economic system, the sanctity of private property, an emphasis on self-reliance in the social sphere, and a general reverence for the 19th Century tradition of independence and rugged individualism became part of the status quo with which many evangelicals could most easily identify. The virtues of free enterprise and self-reliance were extolled alongside the preaching of personal salvation through faith in Christ.

While this was the status quo, and still is, for numbers of people in Western society, the society as a whole has witnessed a dramatic shift of the status quo in the 20th Century.

What is the present-day status quo in the free Western nations, and specifically in the United States? When one looks at the populace of the United States, there are, of course, wide divergencies—the determined conservatism of the Deep South, the agrarian individualism of the Midwest, the doctrinaire liberalism of the Eastern Seaboard. However, at the level of official and non-official authority, the status quo is much less diverse.

In his philosophical analysis of American liberalism, James Burnham points out that "since some time in the 1930's liberalism has been the prevailing American public doctrine, or ideology. The predominant assumptions, ideas and beliefs about politics, economics, and social questions are liberal. I do not mean that a large majority of the population is, by count, liberal. Perhaps a majority is liberal, but that is hard to determine accurately. What is certain is that a majority of those who control or influence public opinion is liberal, that liberalism of one or another variety prevails among the opinion-makers, molders, and transmitters: teachers in the leading universities—probably the most significant single category; book publishers; editors and writers of the most influential publications; school and college administrators; public relations experts; writers of both novels and nonfiction; radio-TV directors, writers and commentators; producers, directors and writers in movies and the theater; the Jewish and non-evangelical Protestant clergy and not a few Catholic priests and bishops; verbalists in all branches of government; the staff of the great foundations that have acquired in our day such pervasive influence through their relation to research, education, scholarships, and publishing."[13.]

The culture in which the church lives in the 1970's has been significantly shaped by the political and social doctrines of liberalism. Social and governmental institutions, legal theory, economic policy, education, international relations—many of the areas in which Christians have social concern—are today predominantly liberal at the official level. In a word, liberalism is the status quo.

One may judge this to be good or bad, depending upon

his personal experience or persuasion. For our purposes, we simply note it as a fact of existence, so that we may see more precisely the situation in which the church stands as she faces social issues.

Insofar as the church simply lines up unthinkingly with the latest issue dictated by the secular establishment, she stands in danger of surrendering her distinctive witness, becoming a mere yes-man for the secular culture.

That this danger is more than mere conjecture can be readily ascertained by noting the monotony with which the agendas of church conventions parrot the latest issue or crisis in the secular scene.

When "ecology" was suddenly elevated from an obscure branch of biology to the status of a political slogan, church officials dutifully added it to the agenda of "crisis issues" (though their members had already been inhaling near-lethal doses of smog for better than two decades). The latest thrust of the secular establishment in civil rights, economic policy, or social welfare will almost inevitably find an answering echo in some church publication or pronouncement within two or three weeks.

Even a cursory reading of religious publications reveals a distinct tendency on the part of church officialdom to parrot the pronouncements and programs of the liberal status quo, the secular establishment. We do not judge this to be either "good" or "bad" in itself; such a judgment would have to be made in each individual situation. But a tendency to become too closely intertwined with the secular establishment poses a danger about which history, from the time of Constantine, would sound a note of warning.

A charismatic approach to social action seeks to remain free of entanglement with a secular status quo, whether conservative or liberal. It recognizes the sovereignty of the Spirit, which may offer fresh ways of recognizing needs, and creative ways of ministering to those needs, that go alike beyond the doctrinaire conservatism of the evangelical and the doctrinaire liberalism of the social activist.

Chapter Four

SOCIAL ACTION—JESUS STYLE

The world did not dictate Jesus' agenda. He often responded with compassion to the needs which came across His path, as when He healed the servant of the Centurion, or fed the 5000 in the wilderness. But the need alone did not determine His action. He could thread His way past a whole throng of sick and invalid in the portico of Bethesda, to speak to one paralytic man. When the crowd pressed Him with political intentions, to make Him their king, He withdrew from them. On one occasion He said that an extravagant gift of perfumed ointment was more appropriate than a donation to the poor. Then, on other occasions, Jesus displayed a sensitivity to situations which the society of His day would scarcely countenance — as when He held a leisurely conversation with a woman at the well of Samaria, or went away from the crowds to visit a well-to-do tax collector. He did not take His agenda from the world. He received it from the Father. "The Son can do nothing of his own accord, but only what he sees the Father doing."[14.]

A charismatic approach to social issues cannot be dictated by the prevailing status quo. Like Jesus, the church must remain open to a wider range of options.

The now-famous story of David Wilkerson, and his

ministry to teenage gangs in New York, was not cribbed from any textbook of social theology. Even today, in spite of evident success in dealing with drug addicts, his work is often dismissed in professional circles, because, as he himself reports, "I don't follow their methods."[15.]

The Church of the Redeemer (Episcopal), in Houston, Texas, has undertaken a ministry of social concern, astonishing in its concept and execution. Yet some of the issues which hold top priority in the religious media raise scarcely a ripple of interest among them. And things which have generally been relegated to the periphery of social action programs, such as worship and Bible Study, are regarded as absolutely central, precisely to their ministry of social concern.

"A worshipping community was an absolute necessity for our personal and corporate stability," said Graham Pulkingham, the man who led the Houston experiment.[16.]

A charismatic approach to social issues does not limit itself to a narrow list of issues, dictated by the secular establishment. Amidst all the clamor of the social arena, it seeks above all else to remain sensitive to those concerns which the Lord Himself sets before His Church.

There is a beautiful phrase in the Song of Solomon: The Bride speaks to the Bridegroom and says, "Draw me after you."[17.] How well she knows her place. How well she has learned her courtly manners! Hers is not to lead, not to direct — but to 'be drawn.'

The Bride of Christ must learn that she can only go somewhere when Her Lord is leading the way. How much damage has been done the cause of Christ by a church which has said, in effect, "Come, Lord, follow us. See how much there is to be done. Come — bless *our* work."

In Matthew 9:36, Jesus saw a great need: "The crowds

were harassed and helpless, like sheep without a shepherd." It tells us that "he had compassion for them." He cites the need to His disciples: "The harvest is plentiful, but the laborers are few." But note carefully His next step. He does not say, "Now plunge into this harvest field, Peter, James, John, and all the rest of you! Identify yourself with these people, in their misery and need! Get the message out to them, for the time is short! Organize a crash evangelism-training program among the other disciples!" No, He says rather: "Pray therefore the Lord of the harvest to send out laborers into his harvest." *Urgency begets urging.*

When we see a need, or have a deep desire, our first step must be an *urging of the Lord.* It dare not be direct action aimed at meeting the need or fulfilling the desire. For then we run the great risk of building *our* kingdom rather than *His* Kingdom.

Erwin Prange, writing from long experience as an inner-city pastor, says, "Too often, when the church tries to become relevant, it becomes secularized and drifts into humanism. Too often we come up with what we think is a great program. We ask the Spirit to bless it, but He says, 'It wasn't My idea in the first place. Why didn't you ask Me in the beginning?' *Relevance begins with God.*"[18.]

It is all too easy to drift away from this clear testimony of Scripture and be guided by pious slogans. How often we have been duped by this slogan: "The need constitutes the call." All one has to do in order to be doing God's will is to take a general principle of Scripture, find a place where it can be applied, and go to work! And then, when you have a good work going, you can begin to shame other Christians who are blind to the need of their fellowman, so settled and complacent; if you do it well enough, you will probably drum up some dollar-support for your work. And no one will ever embarrass you with the fundamental question, "Did the *Lord* lead you into this work? Did *He* initiate it?" For we have accepted the slogan, "The need constitutes the call." Urgency is translated directly into action, without so much as a 'by your leave' to the Lord. When the work is thoroughly planned and under way, we usually glance backward over our shoulder and say, "Oh Lord, come now and bless *our* work."

The crux of this problem lies in the fact that a great many Christians today do not believe in or reckon upon the genuine guidance of the Holy Spirit. They have a sense of duty, but no sense of definite divine direction. They are left with seemingly no alternative but to take the general principles of Scripture and apply them as intelligently as possible.

Certainly there are many places in life where we must use "our sanctified common sense." This is especially true in some of the everyday, routine decisions of life whereby one *carries out* a broader mandate which God has already clearly revealed.

An event in the Book of Acts typifies this beautifully. When Peter was led out of prison by the direct intervention of an angel, he simply followed the angel. Once out of prison, the angel left Peter. "And Peter came to himself, and said, 'Now I am sure that the Lord has sent his angel and rescued me from the hand of Herod and from all that the Jewish people were expecting.' When he *realized* this, he went to the house of Mary..."[19.] In other words, following a direct and decisive leading of the Lord, Peter makes a routine decision based on his own reasoning. The direct leading of the Lord in this case came through the angel. We should not miss the typological significance of this because of the unusual character of the historical event. Even in Scripture, angels appear only rarely to lead God's people. But supernatural guidance itself is commonplace — through signs and wonders, visions and prophecies, dreams, significant events. The Bible clearly indicates that it is not sufficient for an action to be generally "good" in itself, conforming to a general principle of Scripture: Unless it is *initiated by God* it can have no hope of divine approval.

It was the overall will of God for the children of Israel to conquer the Land of Canaan. In Numbers 13:1, the Lord initiated a plan for His people to move into Canaan; they were first of all to spy out the land. But a majority of the spies came back and reported that they would never be able to conquer the land. It was too well manned and fortified. This displeased the Lord. He was ready to lead them into the land with signs and miracles, just as He had led them out of Egypt.[20] When the people realized that the anger of the Lord was roused against them, they thought it could be set right if they would simply move in according to the original plan. This, however, was the product of their human reasoning. It was not the leading of God. Their sin of unbelief had changed God's plan. Now, as they went in, it was not in faith but in presumption: "They *presumed* to go up to the heights of the hill country . . . and the Canaanites . . . came down and defeated them."[21]

A work might be good in itself. It might conform perfectly to general Scriptural principles. It might be a much needed work. It might lie directly at hand. And yet, if it is not the *specific* will of God, it is presumption to enter into it. For there are many "good" works one could do. Anyone with half-open eyes can look around and see scores of situations where general Biblical principles could be applied—more than he could accomplish if he were to spend a lifetime at it. If he were to follow the slogan, "The need constitutes the call," he would soon be a nervous wreck. It is not the goodness or necessity of a work which determines whether we can enter into it, but whether it is the *specific will of God for us to do it at this time.*

There were people in Asia who had never heard the Gospel. To bring them the word of life was certainly a good work, consistent with the Great Commission. Yet Paul did not go to Asia, for the Holy Spirit forbade him. Again, there were people in Bithynia who needed the Gospel. Paul attempted to go there. But then he drew back, because the Spirit of Jesus did not allow him. In the night Paul had a vision. "A man of Macedonia was standing beseeching him and saying, 'Come over to Macedonia and help us.' And when he had seen the vision, immediately we sought to go into Macedonia, concluding that God had called us to preach the Gospel to them."[22.] Many good and necessary works beckoned to Paul. But, sensitive to the leading of the Holy Spirit, he quietly rejected them one by one until the *specific will of God* was revealed to him.

This is no harsh command imposed upon the church. It is the cry of her own heart, "Draw me after you!" Her desire is to be where her Lord is. She has learned, perhaps through painful experience, that when *she* does the leading, the Lord is often left behind. And so she has learned to "wait on the Lord," to do nothing without the assurance that He is indeed drawing her after Himself.

When the Lord does lay a social concern upon the heart of His people, what kind of program should be designed to carry it out? In one sense, a charismatic approach to this phase of social action would also remain open to a wide range of options. We cannot limit the way in which Jesus might work in any given situation. And yet the Lord Himself, in Scripture, has revealed certain principles which suggest how He intends His church to make an impact upon society.

Architects of social concern have proposed a wide-ranging variety of programs to deal with the problems which appear on their agenda: Unilateral disarmament, civil rights legislation, poverty programs, urban renewal, abolition of the death penalty, gun control laws, etc. As varied as these programs are, a common thread runs through them all. It is summed up in the central dogma of contemporary social theology: *We must change the STRUCTURES OF SOCIETY.*

No one will argue that some of the structures of society do not need changing. The question is, how shall they be changed? More specifically, for our purposes, what part shall the church play in bringing about change? What does the Lord want His church to be and do in society?

Part of the problem has arisen from the attempt to answer this basic question in too simplistic a fashion. Much of social theology has been little more than a rationalistic working out of the command to love one's neighbor, and this often in an almost crudely materialistic sense. Armed with the general principle, we charge into the social arena with the banner of Good Intention flying high, spot a solid, objective, measurable need, and proceed to do our good thing. When it is all done — or, if we get bogged down in mid-course — we look back over our shoulder and invite the Lord to tag along and bless our work.

A charismatic approach to social issues would first want a more detailed consideration of the general direction of New Testament thought in this whole regard. While it does not touch on many of the specific issues which confront us today, Scripture nevertheless does provide a sense of the outline and shape which our service for the Lord will take on, if it is biblically oriented.

We would suggest three reference points, three themes, which help delineate the shape of New Testament thought in regard to the church's role in society: (1) "Spiritual

Warfare"; (2) "Separation From the World"; (3) "The Household of Faith." In the next three chapters we shall look at each of these themes in turn, and consider some practical ramifications for the church today.

Chapter Five
THE WEAPONS OF
OUR WARFARE

In his book, *The Satanward View,* James Kallas points out that spiritual warfare between Christ and Satan is a dominant concept in Pauline theology. The *Christus Victor* motif accounts for an astonishing 80% of the salvation passages in Paul, while but 20% take up the forgiveness-reconciliation motif.[23.] In an earlier book, Kallas demonstrates that this same kind of emphasis also characterizes the synoptic Gospels. The concept of spiritual warfare profoundly affects the whole New Testament understanding of the place of the church in the world.

When we talk about the church's involvement in "the world," we must begin by recognizing that our 20th Century cosmology* is significantly different from that of the New Testament. By "world" we mean something rather different from what the New Testament means.

The New Testament writers took seriously the material world, and in this they were not too different from any of us. A disinterest in or abhorrence of "matter" is alien

---

Cosmology is the study of the nature of the world, or the universe. 20th Century man has a substantially different view and understanding of the world than did the man living at the time of Christ. The notion that our view is "right" is rooted more in intellectual conceit than in a sober analysis of the question.

to biblical thought. The Church's early rejection of gnosticism illustrates this in a signal way. While their understanding allowed for a somewhat freer play of supernatural forces in the events of the physical world, and their scientific exploration was less advanced than ours, they were, nevertheless, no strangers to what we could call "the laws of nature." The order of the heavens, the regularity of seedtime and harvest, the functioning of cause-and-effect in natural events was a part of their everyday experience, which they took quite for granted. The very category of "miracle," which plays so significant a role both in the Old and New Testament, only takes on significance against the background of an ordered cosmos.

The fact that they had a theological rationale for events taking place in the physical world, however, still is not the essential point at which they differ from 20th Century man. One could come up with any number of present-day scientists who also believe that the physical world is God-created and God-sustained, including some who have no particular problems with the category of "miracle." Indeed, a rigid rule of material cause-and-effect seems less a dogma in the scientific community today than among certain outdated theologians whose cosmology is still picnicking in Sir Isaac Newton's apple orchard. The real difference between New Testament and 20th Century cosmology relates only incidentally to the physical universe. The significant distinction is their totally different understanding of a non-physical dimension of reality. In a word, the New Testament takes such a dimension of reality with dead seriousness, whereas the 20th Century has largely dismissed it as unreal or inconsequential.

Morton Kelsey, of Notre Dame University, points out this distinction in his little monograph, "Angels, Demons, and other Spiritual Entities."

"'Certainly you are not going to suggest that the world

of demons and angels is worth serious consideration,'"
writes Kelsey, anticipating the mind-set of any typical
20th century audience. "'Everyone knows that these were
just superstitions, concocted out of whole cloth in men's
minds, and our modern scientific enlightenment got rid
of such notions. Why would we want to turn back to the
dark ages when we are free at last from believing in
magic?' And to answer such an objection," Kelsey continues, "I would say quite simply that the idea of a spiritual realm does deserve serious consideration, quite
apart from magic; and it has received such consideration,
sometimes too realistically, in almost every culture in
every age with the exception of our own—the culture of
Western Europe and America since the Enlightenment.

"There is good reason why enlightened Westerners
have turned away from their belief in a realm of spiritual
reality. The first reason was probably a reaction to the
witch-burning of the 18th Century. A second cause was
the positivism of Comte and the growing materialism of
our time. Probably the actual reason most people today
cannot believe in angels or demons is that modern Western man has let his ability to know, his science, mislead
him into doubting the existence of any reality which he
cannot touch or understand. Non-material reality, then,
cannot exist. The creed which underlies this point of view
can be stated rather plainly: There is only matter and
law. Our psyche is nothing but a manifestation of matter.
With our reason we can reach law and with our sense
experience we can reach matter, but there is no faculty
with which we reach any realm of spiritual reality. Since
our psyche is nothing but a manifestation of matter, it
cannot exist independent of matter, and therefore there
can be no spiritual beings like us. We are unique, just an
evolutionary accident, and not a very important one
at that.

"The Christian in the midst of this world view finds himself in a somewhat awkward position. It is true that he believes in matter. This much is legitimate. He also believes in reason, and so he may believe in a rational and theoretical God who has made this matter and may influence it through some unknown agency. He may even reach out to this theoretical God, but only in a rational way. He does not touch Him by experience. Just try experiencing the reality of a theory with no laboratory test tubes or Bunsen burners. Just so, the reality of a soul as a living, vital center is therefore very difficult to hang onto. It becomes a metaphysical principle instead of a feeling, experiencing center. Modern man is largely denied a real soul, for he cannot admit into his life a soul which can touch and experience a vast realm of non-physical reality.

"The New Testament, on the contrary, gives us no such narrow world view, but a very clear picture of two worlds which impinge upon each other. There is a world of matter, and also a world of spiritual reality which includes God, the devil, angels, demons, good as well as evil and unclean spirits, principalities, thrones, powers, dominions, authorities, and beggarly elements. The human being is caught between these two worlds and participates in both of them. This second realm is an experienceable world and is met in dreams, visions, and spiritual encounters of various kinds. But even when we are not aware of this world, the beings in it influence us men, usually pricking us spitefully with physical or mental illness, or sin.

"One of the prime objects of liberalism, theologically, has been to expunge such decrepit nonsense from the fabric of the Christian faith. So we are faced quite directly with the question of what we are to do with this aspect of the New Testament. Does it have any validity for our time? Does it speak truth, or is it merely superstition which ought to be discarded?

"Two things seem to be certain. If all the passages about spiritual entities and the references to them must be removed, this strikes at the validity of the whole gospel narrative, and the authority of the evangelists as well. The New Testament then becomes little more than an interesting and highly elevated literary document. In addition, if we discard the belief in the reality of spiritual beings, we cut ourselves off from the probability of real contact with a real God and we diminish the possibility of believing in a real soul.

"It is my belief," Kelsey concludes, "*that the understanding of spiritual realities which we find in the New Testament is quite consistent with both good sense and actual experience of any real breadth. The world view of the New Testament is a good deal closer to the true nature of the world we live in than the coldly rationalistic and materialistic science which begins by ruling these things out as none of its affair, and ends with an aside out of the corner of the mouth, 'Look, we have proved they don't exist.'*"[24.]

The time is past when the cosmology of the New Testament can be dismissed by a superficial appeal to intellectual snobbery. It is simply too tied up with the essential message of the New Testament to be so easily discarded. In his book, *God and the Unconscious*, Victor White points out that we cannot properly understand the New Testament unless we recognize the central significance which it assigns to the realm of non-physical reality.

"In the pages of the New Testament, Satan and the devils may be said to be fairly ubiquitous from the beginning to the end. The polite efforts of nineteenth century liberal criticism to exorcise the demons from the New Testament, to explain away its more 'devilish' passages as a later and superstitious adulteration of the pure ethical milk of the Gospel, or at least to apologize for them as an unimportant concession to contemporary illusion, have proved a dismal failure. Even the most radical criticism of *Formgeschichte* holds that these passages belong to the most primitive strata, the essential core, of the evangelical tradition. Especially since Schweitzer and Otto, it has become difficult to read the Gospels at all otherwise than as an account of the struggle between the *de jure* Reign of God and the *de facto* reign of Satan – the actual 'prince' or 'god' of this world over human hearts, minds, and affairs. 'The devil,' Tertullian will say, with customary exaggeration and insight, 'is fully known only to Christians.' The coming of Christ itself evokes the spirit of antichrist; only when the full light shines in the darkness is the intensity of the darkness made manifest. Not only the words and actions of Christ as related in the Gospels, but also the Epistles, and still more obviously the Apocalypse, are largely unintelligible except on the supposition of the reality and activity of Satan and other malevolent spirits."[25.]

If we want to talk in the same breath about serving the Lord and serving the world, we will have to discard some of our modern day prejudices, and seriously try to come to terms with Jesus' understanding of the world. Writing in the same vein, Kelsey says, "Most modern, educated Christians have been brought up and taught to believe that Jesus' concern with the realm of the angelic and the demonic was determined simply by the naive world view of His own century and by His being caught in it. It was a contemporary illusion, and therefore we must just dismiss this aspect of His ministry! At a recent conference of clergymen, when I proposed to discuss the subject of the angelic realm, exactly this objection was raised, and then suddenly the objector said, 'Yes, I see. I have simply *assumed* that my world view was the correct one, and that of Jesus was incorrect—really without ever critically examining one against the other.' It is my purpose to show that when we reject the idea and experience of the angelic and demonic as only Jesus' concession to the illusion of the first century, it is *we* who are being quite naive. What we are in fact doing is rejecting as illusion everything which mankind has thought except the attitudes and beliefs of Western Europe and America since the mid-18th Century. Isn't it just possible that the most neurotic and upset peoples the world has ever seen may be off on the wrong foot? This part of the world, which has caused more destructive war and chaos in 50 years than we can find in all the rest of history may be just ignorant, having overlooked an important half of life."[26.]

It is precisely this 'other half of life'—this non-physical dimension of reality—which we must take into account, if we wish to appreciate the thrust of New Testament social thought.

Imagine someone sitting down on a Monday evening with this question before him: "What does the church have to say to the pressing social issues of our day?" He picks up a Bible and reads through the four Gospels in a single sitting. The next evening he plows through *Acts* and *Romans.* Wednesday it's the two *Corinthian* epistles, *Galatians,* and *Ephesians.* By the end of the week he's finished *Revelation.*

The next Monday night he sits down with the latest issue of *Christian Century.* Tuesday evening he skims through some back issues of *Commonweal* and *The Lutheran.* He goes on to survey most of the major religious periodicals, as well as some church-related articles in the secular press, always with a view to the question, "What does the church have to say about social issues?"

Any impartial comparison of these two weeks of reading would reveal that the answer of the New Testament to this question appears to be significantly different from the answer which one generally encounters in current religious literature.

In current religious literature, one sees advocated an active, programmed, wide-ranging involvement in the affairs of society. The actions not only of the church, but also of secular and governmental institutions, are scrutinized. The faithful are urged to become involved, to let their witness be felt, their voice be heard, along specific lines of social concern; or, the secular and governmental authorities are addressed directly, through the editorials and opinions of ecclesiastical officials. In a word, the church in the 20th Century advocates active involvement in the affairs of society; she feels called upon to let her voice be heard, her counsel weighed, in the power-centers of society.

By contrast, the New Testament seems to betray but scant interest in the affairs of society. The predominant concern of the New Testament writers is, quite simply, the Gospel; not merely as a spoken message, but as a dynamic activity of God by which He constitutes a new eschatological community. *It is the faith and life of this community which consumes the energies of the New Testament writers.*

To be sure, this community, existing as it does in the world, must arrive at some kind of a *modus vivendi* with society. Both in the Gospels and the Epistles we find more-or less *ad hoc* references to such things as taxes, slavery, imprisonment, respect for civil authority. A somewhat more active concern for helping people in need, usually on a person-to-person basis, is found in some of the sayings of Jesus, or in the apostolic admonition to "do good to all men."[27.] But such references stand on the periphery of New Testament thought.

The overriding theme of Jesus' preaching and ministry was the Kingdom of God, and the people who were being called into it. The manifest concern of the Epistles is not for the well-being of the world, but for the well-being of the churches of God.

Hans von Campenhausen, in his definitive study, *Tradition and Life in The Early Church,* points out that "the crucial interests in the life of early Christianity were plainly of a fundamentally different kind [than those espoused by current social theology], and not such as to further any participation in civil and political life. Jesus did not allow the misconception of Himself as a reformer or advocate of a program, either in the ecclesiastical or political sphere. Jesus called men to God. In current and ephemeral questions He declined to become involved.

"Paul's ethical teaching is wholly defensive in character, with its wish to avoid entanglement and friction with the world, and *aiming at social autonomy rather than social integration.* In Luke's writings the political innocuousness of Christianity is emphasized over and over again. In the New Testament, no attention is paid to public institutions as such, but only to Christian conduct toward them."[28]

When Paul, for instance, tells his congregations to pray for the secular authorities,[29] the idea of a Christian penetration of society, with a view to improving its institutions and social structures, is foreign to his thinking. His concern, quite simply, is to strengthen the church: a) by fostering a political climate which will be hospitable to the Faith, and b) through the possible conversion of some of the secular officials.

Jesus' apparent lack of concern for human poverty has often been remarked. Perhaps He was not intimidated by it, being poor Himself. Some of His sayings seem almost to exalt poverty as a surer way into the Kingdom.[30] When some of His followers criticized Mary for expending a whole jar of perfumed ointment on Him, rather than giving the money to the poor, Jesus retorted, "You always have the poor with you " — and went on to say that this incident would become a part of the preaching of the Gospel.[31.] The primary concern, as always, is the Gospel, and the people whom it summons together.

How are we to understand this apparent lack of concern for social issues which we find in the New Testament? Beneath a veneer of pious abstractions (love, peace, righteousness, justice), do we in fact have an unbridled chauvinism in the early church? Having found new life in Christ, do Christians then turn their back on the world and proceed to cultivate their own piety?

If we have no other cosmology, no other *Weltanschauung*, than the materialism and naturalism of the 20th Century, this is precisely the kind of conclusion to which we are driven and we ought to be candid enough to admit it. The discontinuity between New Testament thought and the bulk of 20th Century social theology is simply too blatant to ignore.

For the most part, Christian theology has avoided this issue. Unwilling to re-examine their cosmological presuppositions, and equally unwilling to follow out the implications of a straightforward New Testament exegesis, modern social theorists have come up with an ersatz theology. It is not cut from the fabric of the New Testament, but is pieced together from scraps of 18th and 19th Century Idealism, and scientific humanism. Taking a few passages of Scripture out of context, such as the parable of the Good Samaritan, they have erected a theology of social concern which no more needs Christ as its determinative center than did the laws and regulations of the Pharisees, to which it bears no small resemblance. It is moralistic through and through, destitute of the dynamic of the Gospel. If our social theology is to root itself in New Testament thought, we must undertake a serious re-examination of our 20th Century cosmology.

When we understand "the world" as Jesus and the Apostles did, their apparent disinterest in society begins to make sense. The world, as they saw it, was a world at war. Nothing to do with the little skirmishes which the Roman legions engaged in periodically. Cosmic war. *Spiritual* war. Light against darkness. Good against evil. Christ against Satan. Events in the visible realm were but symptoms of a titanic struggle going on in the "heavenly places" of the invisible realm.

Writing to the Colossians, Paul portrays Christ as "disarming the principalities and powers" through His death on the Cross.[32] He sees this warfare being continued through the ministry of himself and the other Apostles, as they, with divine power, destroy Satan's strongholds.[33] To tinker around with a dislocation in the physical world, without getting at the root of it in the spiritual realm, would be akin to treating a multiple bone fracture with a band-aid. The world is under attack, worse yet, in bondage. "The whole world lies in the power of the evil one."[34] Unless and until this problem is dealt with, no amount of social engineering will have any lasting effect on the world.

The New Testament's seeming lack of interest in social issues is therefore not rooted in indifference, but in a particular *battle strategy*. While modern social theologians would opt for a measure of improvement in men's immediate circumstances, Jesus and the Apostles envisioned nothing less than their total deliverance from the dominion of evil.

Why did much of the social activism of the 1960's end in disillusionment? How are we to account for the apathy which has overtaken many of the people and programs which started out with such high purpose and resolve a few years ago? A peace or civil-rights march, which would have marshalled tens of thousands of placard-carrying adherents in 1966, has a hard time drumming up enough support to rate back-page coverage today. The angry young men of the 1960's have become the disillusioned and often embittered men of the 1970's.

A young man who had been active in the social revolution of the 1960's put his finger on a key factor of this phenomenon at the Notre Dame Catholic Charismatic Conference in 1972: "We were angry and determined young men. We wanted to see justice done. But we had a lesson to learn, a hard lesson, and it was this: 'The anger of man does not work the justice of God.'"[35.]

Human indignation, no matter how "righteous," is no adequate weapon for dealing with satanically instigated injustice. Worse, it actually plays into the hands of the enemy. Satan laughs at our demonstrations, our fumbling attempts at setting the world right, when it is powered by nothing more than human indignation and resolve. For it saps our energies without ever threatening his position and power. We quell an injustice here, only to see something worse erupt over there. We are like beleagured firemen, running frantically to put out fires, with never a thought of coming to grips with the pyromaniac who goes around setting off the fires.

The most disturbing feature about today's social activists is not the issues they raise, nor even some of the things they do, but the *spirit* in which it is done — the mood of uncritical self-righteousness, and of unbridled anger toward those who oppose them, or who do not share their point-of-view. This virtually insures the failure of their plans. For it ignores the spiritual dimension of the conflict. We cannot wage spiritual warfare with the weapons of this world.

What kind of armor and weapons *are* effective in spiritual conflict? Paul details some of them in Ephesians 6:10-18: truth, righteousness, the gospel of peace, the hope of salvation, faith, the word of God, prayer. The world looks on such things as pious platitudes. The Apostles knew them for their power — power not merely to deal with visible symptoms of evil, but power to bring down the very strongholds of evil.

It is against the background of this kind of understanding that an emphasis on *spiritual gifts* gains added significance. Such gifts as wisdom, knowledge, healing, miracle, discernment of spirits hold out the potential for dealing with problems in a way that goes beyond traditional social activism. Why settle merely for political or economic action, if divine power is available for dealing with a problem?

In an Eastern Bloc country, the mayor of a small town began to cast envious eyes on a Christian retreat center. He concocted rumors to blacken their reputation with government authorities. He succeeded in curtailing their work and outreach. He began to circulate petitions against them, hoping finally to force their closure, so that he could take over their property and turn it into a state-run retirement home — a big feather in his cap with the communist authorities. A clear case of injustice.

What should a Christian do? Organize a demonstration? Write a Letter to the Editor in the local paper, pointing up the injustice? Defy the restrictions which had already gone into effect, have a sit-in? Move in and occupy the mayor's office, and refuse to leave until he sets the situation right? It doesn't take much imagination to picture what any of these tactics would have led to, given the country and setting.

How *did* Christians handle this situation? They complied with all the restrictions, making no complaint. And they began to pray. Their leader spent all of one night in prayer. And at the end of it he was given a vision of their property surrounded by a band of angels. So convinced was he of the genuineness of the vision that he shared it with his co-workers, and expressed confidence that the Lord was going to protect them.

A series of strange events began to unfold. A communist druggist in town became peeved with the mayor, and complained to higher authorities that his vendetta against the retreat center was groundless. Workers in the local factory likewise began to take issue with the mayor, and withdrew their names from his petition. Not many days later the mayor appeared at the retreat center, hat in hand, apologizing for the inconvenience he had caused them, and lifting all restrictions.[36.]

Spiritual warfare, spiritual strategy, spiritual weapons, spiritual victory — issuing in concrete, visible results. This kind of thing could never happen, were not the dimension of *spiritual warfare* taken into account.

A classic social activist, even if he were to accept the validity of such things as prayer and visions and divine intervention, might well dismiss this incident from an iron curtain country as irrelevant to churches in the free world. For in the West, we *can* write Letters to the Editor, organize protests, influence legislation, make our voice heard.

But consider the implications of such a line of reasoning. For one thing, it suggests that we have no theology or basis for Christian social action in a non-democratic society. Our only word to brethren living under those regimes would be to hang on and hope — hope that somehow they will get a democratic regime so that they, too, can begin to exert an influence on their society.

But, more fundamentally, it posits an altogether wrong base for Christian social action. If our social action rests simply on the benign tolerance of the government which happens to be over us at the moment, then it rests on altogether too shaky a foundation. The very silence of many social activists regarding social issues in communist countries betrays their lack of an independent Christian base of thinking. They are captive to the status quo. The current status quo allows for outward social action, so they advocate outward action. If the mood of the secular authority should change, if direct action were forbidden as it is in the East, then social action would presumably be set aside. Then we would "just have to pray."

The point is, that even in the West, where we still have a greater measure of political freedom, "just praying" needs to become central to the whole enterprise of Christian social action. By having the door of outward action closed to them, these Christians in the East were forced to move along another avenue of action. Reduced to the weapons of *spiritual* warfare, they came to grips with the problem at a more fundamental level.

"We know," writes another pastor from behind the iron curtain, "that the real enemy is not the State, but the demonic realm, which has been unleashed, and comes against us with all its power."[37.]

The very freedoms which we enjoy in the West can blind us to the real nature of the struggle in which we are engaged. Unless and until we recognize the spiritual dimension of social issues, we will continue to treat symptoms rather than causes.

At critical junctures of American history, prayer and fasting were employed as matters of public policy. In May 1774, for instance, news was received in Williamsburg, Virginia, that the British Parliament had ordered an embargo on the Port of Boston. At once the House of Burgesses of Virginia passed a resolution protesting this act, and setting aside the day appointed or the commencement of the embargo as a day of *fasting, humiliation, and prayer.* In his diary for that day, George Washington wrote: "Went to church and fasted all day." Fasts were proclaimed by Adams and Madison; three times during the trying days of the Civil War, Lincoln proclaimed a day of fasting, humiliation and prayer. In each of these proclamations, one senses the clear recognition that historical events are subject to the overarching rule of divine providence, and that spiritual factors can have a direct effect upon events in the visible world.[38.] To a large extent, this awareness has been lost in our day. We have lost the biblical sense of a God who is alive and active in history.

The reality of spiritual warfare is a determinative concept in the social thought of the New Testament. The validity or urgency of any particular issue in society must always be judged by its potential effect on the spiritual conflict in which the church is engaged. The church can not be content to solve problems. It has a commission to set men free from the power of the devil. Any action in the social arena which is not sensitive to this dimension of the struggle, *or is ignorant of the kind of strategy which one uses in spiritual warfare,* will miss the real thrust and earnestness of New Testament social concern.

In addressing itself to issues of injustice, contemporary social theology has fallen into a stereotyped way of thinking. The response to injustice must be direct and practical. "The Church is the conscience of the state. It should work to eliminate social inequities by exerting pressure and influence on the power structures of society. It should rigorously oppose injustice and oppression at every turn, taking an active role in the struggles of the disadvantaged." Some, though by no means all, would not exclude violence and revolutionary action as viable options for a Christian, in the struggle to attain justice.

No one seriously questions that the church should

manifest Christ's concern for those who suffer. This stereotyped response is simply a method put forward for achieving the goal. It tends to coincide with liberal ideology, the status quo in the secular realm.

A charismatic approach to social issues will not rule out the general thrust of this stereotype. Under certain circumstances, the Holy Spirit might call for direct action by Christians in the social and political arena. A charismatic approach, however, makes this simple point: This is not a foregone conclusion; it will not always, or necessarily, be the case; one must be open to other alternatives as well. Especially, one must be open to counsel from Scripture which moves along different lines altogether. Precisely because all the clamor in our day is for "rights" and "action," a charismatic approach to social issues will patiently consider other dimensions of suffering, and the struggle against it, which are spoken of in the Bible.

In I Peter 2:18-23, we have a passage which is fairly representative of a genre of New Testament witness which deals with the question of suffering and injustice in a fundamentally different way than the present-day stereotype. A charismatic approach to social issues would remain fully open to the kind of counsel which is found here, even though it goes flat against the prevailing attitude in both our secular and ecclesiastical culture.

"Servants, be submissive to your masters with all respect, not only to the kind and gentle but also to the overbearing. For one is approved if, mindful of God, he endures pain while suffering unjustly. For what credit is it, if when you do wrong and are beaten for it you take it patiently? But if when you do right and suffer for it you take it patiently, you have God's approval. For to this you have been called, because Christ also suffered for you, leaving you an example, that you should follow in his steps. He committed no sin; no guile was found on his lips. When he was re-

viled, he did not revile in return; when he suffered, he did not threaten; but he trusted to him who judges justly."

What do you do when other people make your life difficult? Not just people in general, but people who stand over you in some sense, who have a measure of authority over you — government, public officials, the "in" social group (and you're a minority), a husband, parents. How do you react when you find yourself in an uncomfortable situation because of the way people treat you? Is it a time for fighting?

We understand fighting. A man hits you, you hit him back. A man discriminates against you, you resent him and hunt for a chance to get even. A man defrauds you, you haul him into court. Fighting is the normal human response to injustice and suffering. We know it from first-hand experience.

But how many grasp the dynamics of *faith* in a time of injustice and suffering? Many understand it purely in passive terms: You lie down and take it; you're a milquetoast, a doormat. This, however, is not faith, but fatalism. Real faith, faith-rooted-in-Jesus, involves an active response to suffering.

However, much of the "action" begins *in the realm of the unseen*. That is why many people dismiss the reality and significance of this kind of faith. That is why the Roman world took little note of a man being crucified outside Jerusalem about 30 A.D. They saw only a man who quietly acquiesced to a judgment of death. They did not perceive the "action" behind this event of injustice and suffering — indeed, the *warfare* being waged between God and Satan in the realm of the unseen.[39] And what was it that sparked this action? Not fighting at the human level, but faith. "Mindful of God...He *trusted to Him who judges justly."*

We live in an age of great upheavals. Social. Political.

Personal. Economic. The cry of injustice and suffering rises up from many quarters. The American Negro seeks his place in society. So does the American Indian. Students the world over protest and riot against institutions of society and government. The cries of the oppressed filter through the Iron Curtain. Once again, in their long history of suffering, the Jews hear the awesome whispers of "pogrom" from their kin in the Soviet sphere. The poor and hungry of the earth raise their muted cry. The heavily taxed citizen shakes his head in despair at the hand-out philosophy of government bureaucrats. Even lawbreakers add their shrill cry of "police brutality" to the growing cacophony of injustice and suffering.

What shall a Christian do? Is it a time for fighting?

St. Peter wrote to people who were undergoing some of these same things—injustice and suffering. He says that Jesus left us an example, that we should follow in His steps. He outlines five aspects of Jesus' encounter with injustice and suffering, which form a kind of paradigm for His followers—

1. *He was BLAMELESS.* "He committed no sin." He was tempted in every respect as we are, yet without sinning.[40.] He met every situation by relying on the Word of God rather than the words of men or of Satan.[41.] Most especially, He did not allow injustice and suffering to provoke Him into sin.

He was deprived of His rights under Jewish law, mocked and beaten without cause, even robbed of His clothing as He hung upon the Cross. Yet He instigated no rebellion or revenge against the authorities who oppressed Him.

If we follow in Jesus' steps, a first concern will be to remain blameless. We will not allow injustice and suffering to provoke us into sin. The 'righteous indignation' of the flesh rouses easily: The sword whips from the sheath,

and off comes the ear of someone standing nearby, someone perhaps quite innocent of actually perpetrating the
injustice.[42.] Jesus' rebuke of Peter is His rebuke of every
Christian who allows himself to be provoked into sin by
a situation of injustice and suffering.

*Injustice and suffering do not confer upon any person
the right to sin.* The fact that you are poor and someone
else is rich does not confer upon you the right to covet.
The fact that you are hungry and someone else has food
does not confer upon you the right to steal. The fact that
you are oppressed and someone else is free does not confer
upon you the right to pillage, rape, loot, and burn.

Hate and revenge is the normal human response to injustice and suffering. So-called "righteous indignation"
is the same thing, camouflaged beneath a veneer of pious
morality. Satan hopes to evoke this kind of response from
us in a situation of injustice and suffering, *for he knows
that it will destroy us.*

The evil and injustice may be instigated by Satan himself, yet a Christian dare never indulge in reactions and
instincts which are "perfectly normal" for human beings.
If we allow ourselves to be provoked into such reactions,
we act like irrational animals, and the end will be our
own destruction.[43.]

Archie Moore, the black athlete, made this point in the
wake of riots which tore through American cities: "Do we
want to become wild beasts bent only on revenge, looting,
and killing and laying America bare? Hate is bait, bait for
the simple-minded... if we resort to lawlessness, the only
thing we can hope for is civil war, untold bloodshed, and
the end of our dreams."[44.]

2. *He was HONEST.* "No guile was found on his lips."
He did not compromise the truth in order to avoid injustice and lighten His suffering. He stood before the High

Priest and calmly testified that He was the Christ [45.] — knowing that it would bring down the judgment of death upon His head.

Pontius Pilate was inclined to set Jesus free. He said to Him, "Do you not know that I have the power to release you, and the power to crucify you?" Jesus might easily have curried Pilate's favor, and avoided suffering. But He thrust the temptation aside and spoke the truth: "You would have no power over me unless it had been given you from above."[46.]

In a situation of injustice and suffering, we must remain absolutely honest. In other words, while we do not strike out against the injustice and suffering, *neither do we condone it.* You are always "prepared to make a defense to any one who calls you to account for the hope that is in you,"[47.] cost what it may. The mood in which you do this, however, is not militant and aggressive. It is merely a truthful response. The response, Peter tells us, is to be like that of Jesus — gentle and reverent.

Reading some of the literature which pours out of the religious press, one could easily get the idea that the greatest danger which people face in the world today is such things as injustice, poverty, discrimination, hatred, unequal rights and opportunities — to be battled and avoided at all costs. This is far from the mind of Jesus. He guaranteed His followers that they *would* encounter such things,[48] but such things were not regarded as particularly dangerous. The greatest danger which the world faces today, as always, is simply this: *The danger of rejecting Christ.*

In some parts of the world this danger is now open and objective: One is challenged to deny Christ, or face torture and imprisonment, even death. In the free Western nations the danger is more subtle. We are tempted to deny Him on the installment plan, eroding away our faith by the lives we lead (for you can deny Him as much by your life as by your words).

"This tax is not fair, so a little dishonesty is warranted...."

"This situation is too difficult to bear, so you can compromise a bit...."

"It's only a number, after all, and without it you can't buy or sell, and how can you live without food? Surely God wouldn't ask you to put up with such an impossible situation!"[49.]

The most potent response to injustice and suffering is not militant retaliation, but a calm and confident witness to the truth — regardless of the consequences.

3. *He was QUIET.* "When He was reviled, He didn't revile in return." Pilate's soldiers pressed a mock-crown upon His head, stuck a mock-scepter in His hand, and draped a mock-robe around His shoulders. "Hail, King of the Jews!" they said, mocking. He took it in silence. Later, as He hung upon the Cross, the elders of the people mocked Him: "He saved others; he cannot save himself. He is the King of Israel? Let Him come down from the cross and we will believe in Him."[50.] Jesus returned not a word.

In a time of injustice and suffering, we must learn to *guard our words*. This moves us deeper into the dynamics and the mystery of suffering. Jesus said, "Bless those who curse you, pray for those who abuse you."[51.] God works out His purpose in a situation of injustice and suffering. He uses these situations to bring blessings to the oppressor through the oppressed. Seen at the purely natural level, the oppressed appears quite helpless. But seen in spiritual perspective, the oppressed holds a virtually impregnable position *from which to bless his oppressor*. Yet, in order to fulfill this purpose of God, the oppressed must guard his words. For the tongue that curses and reviles cannot also bless."[52.]

Reviling disqualifies us to bless. Had Jesus turned on the robbers who reviled Him with reviling in turn,[53.] He could not have turned to one of them later with words of blessing: "Today you will be with me in Paradise."[54.] Because it is rooted in God, the power of the oppressed to bless is far greater than the power of evil to oppress.

Not only individual Christians, but the church, in her various official bodies and denominations, is far too talkative in the face of injustice and suffering. She needs to learn from her Lord how to behave. "Like a sheep that before its shearers is dumb, so he opened not his mouth."[55.]

Neither Jesus nor His Apostles wasted time offering advice, or levelling moral judgments, toward the "power structures of society." The idea that the church is the "conscience of the state" is a role which the church has arrogated to herself; it is not found in the New Testament. The Apostle Paul specifically says, "What have I to do with judging outsiders? Is it not those inside the church whom you are to judge? God judges those outside."[56.]

There is a perfectly practical reason for this silence toward society, both from Jesus and from the Apostles: The world has no capacity for receiving the word of the church, because it does not have the Holy Spirit.[57.] When the church addresses itself to society in regard to a particular issue in society, that word will inevitably be received as "law," for the structures of the world have no other frame of reference for understanding God. "Grace" is the peculiar understanding vouchsafed to the church. If the church, *qua church,* ignores this fact and offers freely its opinions on any and all matters, the world will react as the world must ever react to "law" — with rebellion.

This talkativeness of the church has helped bring about

the growing indifference and even antipathy which she is experiencing from the world today. She needs to relearn the lesson of the early church. She triumphed not by what she said to the world, but by what she suffered at the world's hand.

4. *He was FORGIVING.* "When He suffered, He did not threaten." The religious leaders plotted against Him. Pilate had Him flogged, then condemned Him. The soldiers crucified Him. Yet His only response to all this was, "Father, forgive them, for they know not what they do."[58.] Jesus knew that His suffering was the very instrument appointed by God for their redemption.[59.] And Peter says that we are to follow in His footsteps.

To follow in the footsteps of Jesus means to share "the fellowship of His sufferings."[60.] A Christian looks upon a time of injustice and suffering not as an occasion for revenge, but for redemption. The example of Jesus is stark indeed: He did not even threaten. He not only refrained from immediate retaliation, but He surrendered all thought of future revenge. (A threat is merely a promissory note of retaliation, to be paid out at some future date when one has the capability.) Does the church have the courage to speak this unpopular word?

The shrill cry for "rights" and "justice" is much heard in the land today. Leaders of church and state alike encourage it. But the apostolic word is more calm, for it sees injustice and suffering at a deeper level. The consistent New Testament counsel to those suffering injustice is not "rebel" but "endure"—for through patient endurance you will not only save your souls,[61.] but will also be the occasion for blessing the very ones who oppress you. Is not this precisely what Christ did, hanging upon the Cross?[62.]

In the midst of the racial turmoil of our land, where is this apostolic word to be heard? One searches in vain for it in religious pronouncements and periodicals. The cry is all for protest, demonstration, rebellion. Do we not recognize that we are involved in more than 'social' conflict, that this is *spiritual* warfare? Have we become so naive in spiritual things that we now think this is the kind of weaponry the Apostle Paul spoke of when he said, "Though we live in the world we are not carrying on a worldly war, for the weapons of our warfare are not worldly but have divine power to destroy strongholds"?[63.] Do we really think that protests and demonstrations have the power to bring down *Satan's* strongholds? Indeed, these very things may well serve to advance Satan's causes — pious phrases and slogans notwithstanding. For that which is born of hate will beget hate in turn, no matter in what deceptive language it cloaks itself; that which is born of rebellion will beget rebellion in turn. The anger of man simply does not bring to pass the purposes of God,[64.] no matter how "justified" a cause may seem in our eyes. It is not words and reason that determine the direction of a movement, but the spirit which initiates it.

Satan has much to gain by introducing a *frenetic spirit* into our social concerns. If he can stir us up to protest and rebellion, we may never become quiet enough to rediscover the one power which will defeat Satan, and set right injustices, and that is the power of Christ to suffer in His Body, the church.

Has the church seriously reckoned with the spiritual potential of Christians caught up in the social upheavals of our day? Has the church any longer the apostolic authority and courage to speak to those who suffer, as did the Apostles Peter and Paul?

"Let all who are under the yoke of slavery regard their masters worthy of all honor[65.] ... take your share of suffering for the gospel in the power of God[66.] ... one is approved if, mindful of God, he endures pain while suffering unjustly.[67.] Or the words of Jesus Himself, "If any one strikes you on the right cheek, turn to him the other also."[68.]

Seen in purely natural terms, power appears to lie on the side of the oppressor. But seen in spiritual perspective the power and initiative lie with the oppressed: Their capacity to suffer, and through suffering to triumph, is as much greater than the power of the oppressor, as the Cross of Christ was greater than the legions of Rome.

The President's Commission on Civil Disorders laid the blame for riots in America at the door of white racism. There may be a large element of truth in this, although it is undoubtedly too simplistic an answer to what is a staggeringly complex problem. Nevertheless, the remedies proposed have been overwhelmingly "law."

The civil law proposed by governmental leaders is to be expected. That is their proper response. But the pious pronouncements of moral law from the church denote a tragic regression from the apostolic word. White racism or black racism will not be healed by law, civil *or* moral. It will be healed, if at all, by suffering. The suffering and deprived Christians in America hold in their very suffering the greatest power for renewal—the power of the Cross as a lived experience.

But do we dare say this? We are too little confident of our stand in the power of the Gospel; too much intimidated by slogans and cliches. The imperious rejoinder whips back: "That's easy enough for you to say, as a white, middle-class American. You'd pipe a different tune if you lived in the ghetto."

Onesimus could have levelled the same kind of an *argumentum ad hominem* at Paul: "It's easy enough for you, Paul, to tell me to go back to Philemon and become his slave again. You're a free-born Roman citizen. You don't know what it's like being subjected to the injustices and indignities of servitude."

If we want to reason and believe and react the way the world does, then we will get the kind of results that the world gets: hate, strife, warfare, bloodshed. If we dare proclaim the Gospel, not because we are equal to it, but because it bears the living Christ into a situation of injustice and suffering, then we may expect to see things that the world will wonder at: Strength out of weakness, hope out of despair, love out of hate, healing out of suffering. The ways of the world and of Satan seem attractively logical. They approach the problem of injustice and suffering head on, with sound moral imperatives. But they conveniently avoid any reference to the real cause which lies behind the injustice and suffering: The power of the Evil One. And the law has ever been his ally.[69.]

It is not law or moral preachment which will heal the deep infirmity in the spirit of Western culture. If healed at all, it will be through the suffering of those who dare give up all threats and follow in the footsteps of Jesus.

5. *He was TRUSTING.* "He trusted to him who judges justly." Jesus commended the entire situation, including His persecutors, to God. Finally, He committed Himself utterly to God.[70.]

This is the *raison d'etre* for entering into a time of injustice and suffering—not just enduring it, but *entering into it,* as Jesus did. In a time of injustice and suffering, we are to *look to God alone.* This is what makes sense of it all. By refusing to fight, by spurning the weapons of this world, we call into action a higher order of weapons. We unleash the power of God. We allow Christ to "fight" for us. For He alone is equal to the power of the principalities and thrones ranged against us.

This does not make "sense," any more than it made

sense for Him, who was to become King of kings, to come into His royal power through an ignominious death upon the Cross. Yet He knew that a mighty, divine "therefore" stood at the end of His trail of suffering: *"Therefore* (because He poured out his soul to death), I will divide him a portion with the great, and he shall divide the spoil of the strong."[71.]

To speak thus is to court misunderstanding. One recognizes the danger of eliciting "agreement" from those with whom a Christian does not agree — those who enjoy the role of privilege, and are happy for any word which will keep the disadvantaged contentedly in their place.

The Apostles faced the same possibility of misunderstanding: Their counsel to "honor the Emperor" certainly could have evoked the rabbinic equivalent of "Quisling!" from patriotic Jews. No matter. Their word went beyond local conditions and situations, beyond personal experience and opinion. They had learned "in whatever state they were to be content."[72.] They had received a revelation which gave them faith and courage to enter into suffering — *and to teach their flocks to do likewise.* Not because they wanted to preserve any status quo, but because God had revealed to them that this was the only way that injustice and evil could ever be dealt with at its root.

Had they preached rebellion, antiquarians today might be able to dig up one more case of man's futile attempt to set the world right by his own efforts. Because they did not go this route, but chose instead to remain faithful to the revelation which they had received, we have today a Word which still dares invite men into the fellowship of His sufferings, there to discover the inmost secret of divine love.

A charismatic approach to social issues must look beyond the immediate or seemingly obvious solution to a problem. Simplistic direct action may miss altogether dealing with the fundamental issues which are involved.

"The solution to men's problems," said a leader of the Ann Arbor charismatic community, "must be a *total* solution, a total meeting of man's needs."[73.]

This means dealing not only with the need that meets our eye, but also with the enemy whom we do not see with our eyes—dealing with him by using "the weapons of our warfare."

Chapter Six
SEPARATE—AND SAVE

It strikes us strange that a church with a concern for the world should separate herself from the world. Yet this is a clear and dominant theme in the New Testament. It flows out of the concept of spiritual warfare. In order to help the world *in the way that Jesus wants the world to be helped*, the church must maintain a certain aloofness from the world.

This goes flat against contemporary social theology. The talk today is all in terms of "involvement," "penetration of society," "being where it's at." Yet the biblical testimony quietly reaffirms, "Do not love the world or the things in the world[74]... escape the defilements of the world[75]... keep yourself unstained from the world[76]... friendship with the world is enmity with God. Whoever wishes to be a friend of the world makes himself an enemy of God[77]... If anyone loves the world, love for the Father is not in him."[78]

Why does God—Who desires to save the world, and has called the church to help in this great work—command the church to separate herself from the world? An illustration may help at this point.

Suppose a man owns a run-down apartment building. Several managers have operated it for him, trying to stay abreast of the repairs, and keep it halfway livable. But finally the owner decides that the only thing to do is to demolish the whole structure, and build a new apartment house on a vacant lot three blocks down the street. The only trouble is, the tenants don't want to move. The old rat-trap isn't perfect, but they're suspicious of the unknown quantity of a new apartment house.

"They say a lot of those new apartment houses have paper-thin walls, and the neighborhood isn't too friendly either, and old things are usually better anyway."

So the owner visits several of the tenants until he finds one family that's willing to move into the new apartment building.

"Just let everyone know how nice it is." That's all the owner asks of them. "If they see that you like it, maybe they'll be willing to move, too."

Of course they have to move out of the old apartment house, bag and baggage. If they sneak back into the old apartment house to sleep, or cook, or have a party every so often, the neighbors are going to suspect that maybe that new apartment building isn't so great after all.

They have to drop by often enough to keep contact with their old neighbors. That is part of the owner's strategy. But they also have to separate themselves, so that the neighbors have no doubt that they intend to stay on in the new apartment house.

The command for this family to become separate makes sense in the light of the owner's ultimate intention. It is in this sense, as a part of His eschatological strategy, that we must understand God's command for the church to become a separate people.

If we take Scripture seriously, we cannot escape the conclusion that God has slated the world for demolition. In historical types, such as the Flood, and the destruction of Sodom and Gomorrah; in selected passages of the prophets, such as the 24th Chapter of Isaiah; in the apocalyptic discourses of Jesus, in which He specifically compares the end of the age to the age of Noah,[79.] and says that the earth will pass away;[80.] or in a passage like 2 Peter 3:19-23, which reflects the general expectation of the primitive Christian community that the earth, at the end of the age, would be cleansed by fire — we see that the Bible points forward to a time when the world, as we know it, will be demolished, in order to make way for a new heaven and a new earth.[81.]

The judgment foreseen is thoroughgoing; judgment of the rebellious angels;[82.] judgment of the peoples of the earth;[83.] finally even including, as in the passages cited above, a purgative judgment of the physical universe itself. Who will survive? The church is God's answer to such a query. She is, in our figure, the new apartment building. Or, to use the biblical figure, she is the ark, which promises safe passage through the time of judgment and destruction coming upon the earth.

The church's separated existence is lived as over against this kind of eschatological expectation. The overriding concern of the Apostles is to build up the church. Not because they are introverted, and neglectful of the world's needs, but precisely out of concern for the world. Unless people are united to Christ, through His Body, the Church, they have nothing to look forward to but destruction and judgment.

To expend great efforts at reforming or improving the structures of society would be like Noah leaving the building of the ark to help some of his neighbors put in the spring planting — a poor stewardship of one's time, detracting from the important work of preparing the ark of safety. The church's primary work is not to help people live a somewhat better life in the old apartment building, but to convince people to move over into the new apartment house.

This is the essential conclusion to which Hans von Campenhausen comes in his study of "The Christian and Social Life According to the New Testament."

"The original link joining Christianity to the world is the command and will to preach Christ. The 'mission' in this sense is, in the first place, the only, and, therefore, the real bridge joining the church to the world. This is what those 'outside' have to know when they turn their attention to the church, so as to prevent any disappointment."[84.]

It is from this perspective that we must understand Jesus' metaphors of 'light' and 'salt.'

"You are the light of the world. A city set on a hill cannot be hid."[85.] The church is seen here not primarily as an agency to improve society in a direct way, but as an *example* to the world of a people among whom God dwells. Their life under God attracts people, as a well lighted city attracts travellers on a dark night. Their most important service is to invite men out of the darkness into the city of light. Their way of life is meant to shine out into the world with such power that men will be drawn away from their darkness, and ask how they, too, can live in the light. The task of the church is not simply to help rearrange the furniture in the hovels of the world, so that people will stub their toes in the darkness less frequently. God wants the church to bring people out of darkness into the community of light—to add them, as living stones, to the household of faith.

Hebrew-Christian evangelist Paul Gordon makes the point that "the expression of Christ in His Body is the key to evangelism. If we allow God to live His life in us, it is like a magnet to draw men to Christ.

"It is a question of first things first. We must let God do His work in us...must *show* Jesus to the world, by our coming together and loving one another."[86.]

One of the powerful trends in modern theology is summed up in the German word *Mitmenschlichkeit*—"togetherness with one's fellow man." According to the trumpeters of this doctrine, the whole experience and purpose of Christianity is to be found through involvement with one's fellowman. "Do you want to find God? Lose yourself in the world of men! Wherever two people encounter one another in love, there 'God' becomes real, there 'Christ' is realized." The doctrine is all the more pernicious because it mixes a great deal of truth with its fundamental error.

It is well to encourage people to be 'the salt of the earth' —to enter into the life of our society with a redemptive purpose. But it is well also to remember Jesus' word of caution: "If salt has lost its taste, how shall its saltness be restored? It is no longer good for anything except to be thrown out and trodden under foot by men."[87.]

How does salt 'lose its taste'? Salt is one of the stablest compounds we have. It can only be broken down by an electrolytic process. Yet salt can lose its taste and did also in Jesus' day. Because it was so precious, salt was often mixed with earth, to make it stretch further. If this was overdone, the salt was stretched so thin that it lost its savor. Better a little salt, concentrated and pure, than a great mass swallowed up and indistinguishable in the earth.

A number of young people now active in Christian charismatic communities came out of the student activist movements of the 1960's. A former SDS adherent said that he came to see the futility of political action. The evils in society are much deeper than they then realized. The people he knew in the activist movements have either quit, got a good job and joined the Establishment, or cracked up mentally. The only ones still doing something in the social arena are those who have come through to a dynamic new faith in Christ.

He has come to see the church's role as that of offering, for those who will accept it, an alternative life style. The life of the Christian community is the essential 'service' which the church has to offer to the world."[88.]

Any effective Christian involvement in the world must proceed from a 'concentrated' community of believers. The church's value to the world is not so much in what she does for the world as in what she *is* in the world. If she spreads herself out, attempting to do a great many things, she may rearrange the world's miseries into slightly more endurable configurations. But if she *is* what God calls her to be — if she is truly a light, truly salt — she will demonstrate to the world how misery itself can be dealt with.

The Achilles heel of modern social theology is its preponderant emphasis upon man's material and social needs. For when we look at sectors of society which have achieved material and social status, we do not see a particularly appealing picture. They, too, are plagued with turmoil, distress, and dissolution. Even if the church could succeed in helping triple the world's standard of material and social welfare, there is no indication that the standard of *life* would be improved. The quality of personal, family, and social life among the affluent does not offer that much by way of encouraging example. The degree to which the drug and drop-out culture is peopled by children of upper-class families suggests that a preoccupation with the comforts and conveniences of worldly existence can reach a point of satiety, of reversal.

A well-to-do couple went vacationing for two weeks in Mexico. Afterward, at a party in their home, they were showing slides and telling about their trip.

"You can't imagine the poverty," commented the wife. "It's indescribable. And yet, the people seem so *happy*."

Someone offered the opinion that perhaps there would be some way of helping them.

"Yes," said one of the men wryly, "then they could become rich and miserable, like us."[89.]

Misery and deprivation are not confined to the ghetto. A charismatic approach to social issues is wary of any program which attempts to minister merely to a person's material needs. The Snob Hills of our culture are too full of their own varieties of addiction and misery to make them the goal of our social action.

The primary calling of the church is not to help provide people with a higher standard of living in the world. Rather, the church calls people to be delivered from slavery to the world-system, and to enter the freedom and security of a new community, God's people, the church.

The church, as a separated community, is meant to be God's example in and to the world — a people who have heard of the destruction which is to come, and have believed in the Savior who has been offered. Her essential message to the world is not, "Can I help you fix up your house?" — but, rather, "Come over, and move in with us." A costly suggestion, as we shall consider in the following chapter.

Chapter Seven
THE HOUSEHOLD OF FAITH

What does the world actually see when it draws near this community? What kind of an example do people see in the household of faith? More specifically, considering our theme, how does this household relate itself to some of the social needs and issues about which the world is concerned?

In the evangelical sector of the church, the world draws near and sees a people who appear to have in common certain *words* – a set of beliefs, a code of behavior, a style of worship. When they have finished exchanging *words* with one another, this people breaks up and each one heads off in his own direction. Thus what the world has come to expect from evangelicals is primarily an offering of *words*. Here and there the words will be underscored and authenticated by the life-style of an individual Christian whom one has come to know. But the predominant impact of evangelicals, *as a body,* is in terms merely of what they *say*.

This is not unimportant. The words which they offer can be life-transforming. But when we observe the growth patterns of evangelical groups, we can only conclude that much of the talk appears to be wasted. Those who hear the words, and walk away, far outnumber those who stay to become part of this word-sharing fellowship.

Because their corporate life centers mostly around words, evangelicals communicate to the world a truncated version of Christianity. Not in what they say, but in what they are, as a group. In words, they may describe the Christian fellowship in glowing terms, as a body of people knit together by close bonds of affection, mutual concern, and helpfulness; a community that answers to the language and imagery of family life. In actuality, except for a few hours of word-sharing each week, they live their lives more or less aloof from one another.

Arthur Richter, well-known evangelical leader and writer in Germany, scores evangelical individualism in his carefully reasoned treatise, *Der Neue Mensch und die Neue Gesellschaft* (New Man and New Community): "The 'new creation' which Christ ushers in is falsely narrowed down to a merely personal experience. The upshot is a private form of Christianity, in which one is happy to be at peace with God, and proceeds to set in order his everyday life. He meets other Christians at Sunday worship services, and contributes his bit toward building up the congregation. His membership in the church is not much different from membership in any other club or service organization, which asks for just a little part of the member's life. They bring a little piety to the enterprise, and gain a little edification, advice, and comfort, so they can go out and make a better go of their thoroughly private lives. The whole conception is false."[90.]

A "brother" or "sister" can be going through hell in splendid evangelical isolation, neither expecting nor receiving any help from the family of believers. If it is a financial crisis, one checks in with the county welfare department. If it is a family problem, there's a counseling service nearby. Emotional disturbances are referred to the psychiatrist. On Sunday one comes around to church, where the "family" shares the word that Christ is all-sufficient, and we are all one in Christ Jesus. An hour later the "family" disintegrates, and it's every man for himself again. The world, as it looks at evangelical Christianity, does not see the kind of *koinonia* described in the New Testament. What it sees is a body of people who as individuals profess complete allegiance to Christ, but who, contrary to Christ's teaching, practice severely limited commitment toward one another.

'The world demands more than nice-sounding theories. It wants a demonstration, proving that the theory works. A millionaire who offers to tell you "how to do it" is more apt to gain a serious hearing than a clutch of college sophomores who have read their first textbook in Economics.

Francis Schaeffer, considering the role of the church at the end of the 20th Century, writes, "We may preach truth, we may preach orthodoxy. We may even stand against untruth strongly. But if others cannot see something beautiful in our human relationships, if they do not see that, upon the basis of what Christ has done, our Christian communities can stop their bickering, their fighting and their infighting, then we are not living properly.

"Our churches have largely been preaching points and activity generators. Community has had little place. I want to see us treating each other like human beings, something that the humanistic student rebels desire but have been unable to produce. Every Christian church, every Christian school, every mission should be a community which the world may look upon as a pilot plant.

"Unless people see in our churches not only the preaching of the truth, but the practice of the truth, the practice of love and the practices of beauty; unless they see that the thing that the humanists rightly want but cannot achieve on a humanist base — human communication and human relationship — is able to be practiced in our communities, then let me say it clearly: They will not listen, and they should not listen."[91.]

In the social action sector of the Church, the world draws near and sees people who appear to have in common certain *causes*. Like the evangelicals, they live the greater part of their lives in separation from one another. But for select causes they pool their efforts, to try to effect certain changes in society.

The motive behind these various causes is not always readily apparent. "Part of our training," said a Roman Catholic layman, who had been active in the social action movement of his church, "was a studied avoidance of any mention of Christ. We were told to do our 'good thing' in such a way that *no one would suspect we were Christians*."[92.]

In the social action movement there has been a decided shift away from an emphasis on "conversion." It is not primarily the individual who needs changing, but the structures of society. This, too, presents a view of Christianity which distorts the biblical message.

The thought of the church changing the structures of society by direct action is alien to the thought-world of the New Testament. Both with Jesus and with the Apostles we find an almost studied avoidance of what we would call political or social involvement. They never lift their voices against Rome, nor are they particularly critical of society, as such. Their counsel for Christians is to respect and obey the secular authorities — the same authorities who had subjugated most of the known world by force of arms, who dispensed justice to non-Romans by fiat or whim, who upheld the institution of slavery as a matter of course, whose chief concern for the poor was the amount of money they could squeeze out of them in taxes. In this kind of a society the church lived, without offering much either by way of advice or complaint.

It was not that they were self-serving supporters of the status-quo. They simply recognized—as too many present-day social theorists do not—that the structures of society will not succumb to a frontal attack by the church. There is a more effective way—the way of *example*.

Evangelicals and social activists have something to learn from each other. But not in the way that is usually meant—that the evangelical becomes more socially involved, and the activist becomes more evangelical. Rather, both need to see the particular place where the other's emphasis can be applied, in order that the church *as example* will make its maximum impact on the world.

What kind of an example *should* the church be to the world? What should the world see, as it draws near the household of faith?

Jesus said, "By this all men will know that you are my disciples, if you have love for one another."[93] *In* the household of faith, the world should see much more than a word-sharing fellowship. It should see a life-sharing fellowship.

If the early Pentecostal movement had continued its initial pattern of racial integration,[94] it may well have changed the face of race relations in the United States. By backing off, and accommodating itself to the standards of the general culture, fellow Christians did a disservice to one another (the impetus for segregation came from black and white alike), and they silenced a testimony which the Holy Spirit wanted the church to make in the world.

Jesus said, "Go and preach the gospel to the whole creation..."[95] *From* the household of faith, the world should encounter more than a series of causes, aimed at reforming society. It should encounter the clear call of the gospel: "Repent, and be baptized every one of you for the forgiveness of your sins; and you shall receive the gift of the Holy Spirit."[96.]

In a sense, evangelicals and social activists have presented an inverted version of Christianity to the world. Social action is something which the world should first and foremost see taking place *within* the households of faith. Word-sharing is something which the world should essentially encounter as *coming out from* the household of faith.

In the short run this can appear introverted and selfish, as though the church were interested primarily in itself, with only words for those outside. But it is rooted in Jesus' concern, which goes so much deeper than man's immediate circumstances.

The life-style of the Christian community is meant to act like a magnet, attracting those outside. At the point of attraction, the church's proper offering is the word of the Gospel, i.e., an invitation to enter the household of faith. For if a man is not drawn into the household of faith, any improvement in his life circumstances will be of but passing moment. He will sink, at last, into final and ultimate misery. Thus, the church must consider a reorientation of its practice, if it is to make a maximum impact upon society.

1) Within the Christian fellowship, it must offer more effective ministry to the practical and social needs of its members. As a by-product, this helps create a climate for the acceptance of the Gospel.

2) In its contact with the world, the church must give first priority to the proclamation of the Gospel. A ministry of social action to the world will always remain a coordinate task of the church.

Instead of looking around for things to do in and for the

world, the church needs first to ask herself how things stand *within* the household of faith. What kind of an example is she living out in the eyes of the world? For it is this that will draw them to *Christ*, and therefore be of any ultimate value.

In 1968, the American Lutheran Church published some interesting statistics about its own membership of some two million people: over 5000 divorces the previous year, 5000 more homes in which either the father or mother had moved out, involving a total of 11,000 children; 3000 illegitimate births (1000 to teenagers); 100,000 families who live in poverty, according to federal standards; 6000 teenagers booked by the police on minor or major offenses; 40,000 eldery living alone, with no family ties, subsisting on an income of less than $2000 a year; 50,000 children under 6 years of age whose mothers are working.[97.] If these figures represent anything like a cross-section of other denominations, the church has a major set of social issues right within the household of faith.

It might reasonably be argued that the church's neglect has compounded the problems which society faces today. A member of Parliament, in England, writing in 1845, long before the advent of the income tax, prophesied that if church members did not pay their regular tithes, and thus take care of the poor in their own midst, then the heavy hand of government would be forced to move in, and would extract more than a tenth of one's income for this very purpose.[98.]

In the area of social welfare, the church has increasingly abandoned its distinctive witness to the world. Contemporary social theology has not only welcomed the intervention of government into the field of social welfare, it has more and more advocated it *as an expression of the Christian faith.*

"The (Christian) citizen who takes seriously his obligation to be his brother's keeper does not begrudge the use of his tax dollars for the alleviation of real need; indeed, he may well take the lead in urging government to expand its welfare services."[99.] This sentence, from a major church publication, represents a fairly typical ecclesiastical attitude toward government welfare programs. There may be some quibbling or complaint about inefficiency, waste, or graft, but no fundamental questioning of the assumption that government welfare programs are a demonstration of Christian compassion and charity.

When government moves in to do something, which the church may also be doing, or which the church may have neglected to do, Christians must recognize a fundamental distinction in the situation. Whereas the church can speak to its members on the basis of a common commitment to Christ, the government cannot. A government welfare program may be argued on pragmatic grounds, but not on the grounds of "Christian principles." For this would involve a compromise of the very nature of the Gospel, by attempting to legislate behavior which, according to the New Testament, must spring from a free response of faith. "For whatever does not proceed from faith is sin."[100.]

A charismatic approach to social issues will not rule out government welfare programs, or a Christian's support of them, *per se.* But neither will it shrink from calling for a more searching inquiry into some of the theological, ethical, and practical implications of the massive government welfare programs, which we have come to take as a matter of course in our day. To the extent that a government welfare program would involve a Christian, however indirectly, in questionable intrusions on the rights of other people, one would seek for alternative methods of ministering to the need in question.

A key aspect of this issue involves the Christian understanding of *property rights.* It has become fashionable to set up an artificial dichotomy between civil or human rights, and property rights, by which the latter obtain an inferior or even negative status. The Bible knows nothing of such a dichotomy. It teaches a marvelously unified concept of justice: The rights obtaining to a man's person are integrally linked to the rights obtaining to his property. In the Ten Commandments, a man's protection from theft (property right) is sandwiched in between his protection from assault (human right) and his protection in judicial proceedings (civil right).

Property rights involve profound spiritual implications. The command against coveting clearly has the protection of property rights in view. But it also involves the gravest spiritual implications. St. Paul says, "Be sure of this, that no immoral or impure man, or one who is covetous (*that is, an idolator*), has any inheritance in the Kingdom of Christ and of God."[101] Coveting is akin or equal to the sin of idolatry. Any welfare program which stirs, however subtly and indirectly, the temptation to covet another man's property, will purchase aid and relief at too dear a price.

The question of government welfare invariably turns on the question of *need.* When this fails to convince a skeptic, the question may be refined to deal with *legitimacy of need.* If it can be shown, for instance, that thrifty, honest, frugal-living people stand in genuine need, then the case for government welfare would seem to be unassailable. Only the "improvident" and "selfish" would stand between such deserving folk and the government purse.

Suppose we accept this extreme position, for the sake of a clearly defined issue: Only the selfish oppose government welfare for needy people. Our responsibility as Christians toward the needy is clear: We must help. But how should we as citizens, and particularly as *Christian* citizens, behave toward those selfish citizens? Do we simply take pleasure in the compulsory nature of taxes, which assures us of having help in our welfare task from the selfish and improvident? In other words, do we *force* the selfish to share their goods with those in need?

The critical moral relationship in the field of welfare today is not between those in need and those who care. You can give as much as you please of your own goods to those in need, through any number of voluntary agencies. The problem, rather, exists between those who care about human need and those who don't. Government welfare is the easy way out for those who care: It forces everyone to join in, and thereby lightens their own burden.

But is it *right*? Can a Christian support it? That is the basic question. Not, "Is this welfare program needed?" (let's assume that it is), but, "Can we in justice force a man to share his goods with those less fortunate?" If you get right down to it, doesn't a man have a right to be selfish with his own goods? And don't Christians have a moral responsibility to protect that right? The commandment does not say, "You may covet another man's goods, providing he is selfish, and you intend to use his goods in a worthy cause." The commandment says flatly: "You shall not covet."

Suppose a community consisted of seven citizens. Two of these are poor, through no fault of their own. Three of the other citizens want to help. The two remaining citizens show no concern whatever. Do the two poor citizens and the three concerned citizens have a right to go up to the two selfish citizens and say, "We have decided that you must share some of your goods with these two poor citizens. You have no choice in the matter. We hold a majority."

This is tyranny and this is theft. And it cannot be equated with a legitimate tax for, say, a new well in the community. The two selfish citizens might object to being taxed for a new well, but they do get tangible return for their money — the use of the well. This would be comparable to the protection a citizen gets in supporting the police force, fire department, national legislature, judicial system, etc. He may not altogether approve of the way his tax money is spent, but in each case he does get a specific return for his tax. This kind of taxation is a 'compulsion' which no sensible citizen has ever quibbled about in principle. But welfare programs do not necessarily return value to the person who is required to support them. They simply confiscate his goods for the benefit of someone else.

A consideration of social welfare which turns on a myopic preoccupation with human need betrays a fundamental misunderstanding of the problem. For the Christian, a more basic issue underlies the whole question of government welfare programs: *Do I, as a Christian, have a right to join in compelling other citizens to become ' their brother's keeper'?* For in voting through a piece of welfare legislation, *the rationale for which is our Christian responsibility toward those in need,* that is what I and my brother-keeping fellow Christians would do: Force all other citizens to become brother-keepers, whether they want to or not. The real choice we are making in supporting such legislation is not between being a brother-keeper or not (we're always free to pursue that on our own); rather, it is between standing for *freedom* or *coercion*.

Charity is integral to the Christian faith. But so is the preaching of the Gospel. By following out the logic for government welfare programs as an expression of Christian charity, we could develop an air-tight parallel case for tax-supported preaching: "It is all well and good to say that children should receive religious instruction from their parents. The fact is that in our day the parents are not doing the job. There are good New Testament reasons for saying that the church should take care of spreading the Gospel. But the church has not done it, at least not on anything approaching the necessary scale — and well over a third of our citizens do not even belong to a church. The citizen who takes seriously his obligation to help spread the Gospel does not begrudge the use of his tax dollars to help accomplish this purpose!"

Here we see the basic issue, with its seductive garb of altruistic principles stripped away. Government welfare programs which are urged on the basis of "Christian principle," are an attempt to accomplish Christian goals by means of *force* or *coercion*. To the man who does not want to be his brother's keeper, we say: "You will contribute to your brother's need whether you want to or not; you will act like a Christian or go to jail." The time is long overdue when we should expose this sentimental propaganda for what it really is: an invitation to tyranny.

A Christian should be moved to compassion — and to action — by the need of his brother. But he should resist any attempt to *force* others to help alleviate that need. For the way of Christ is to take a need upon oneself, not turn a gun or a legal club on someone else and demand that he also take it on.

Those who advocate government welfare programs usually make a common tactical error: They paint the problem of human need so large that nothing short of an omniscient, omnicompetent government can accomplish the task. This is a deceptively simple solution, but it simply is not true.

The government has no magic formula in the field of social welfare. The same techniques of social aid, case work, counseling, vocational rehabilitation and so on, are available to private institutions. The government cannot do a better job. It can merely do a bigger job. For the government has one simple advantage: It can force people to support its program. But such things as tax credits could deal effectively with this aspect of the problem. There are ways of stimulating private initiative which do not infringe on freedom.

Christians must recognize an insidious danger, *for Christians in particular,* in government welfare programs: The dulling of individual responsibility. With an all-powerful Government caring for more and more people, in more and more situations, what happens to Christian conscience, to Christian initiative? The immediate effect is to weaken the ties of love and concern between fellow Christians. Brotherhood does not grow in a vacuum chamber, but in the crucible of daily experience, in suffering and sharing together.

What has happened to congregational life in some European countries? A tax-supported pulpit preaching to empty pews. To force non-Christians to support any phase of Christian work is to cut the nerve of Christian conscience. Asked about the charitable work of the church in Russia, the Archbishop of Moscow replied blandly, "Oh, we have no more need in Russia: the government takes care of it all."[102.]

The picture on the other side can be even more devastating. What happens to our sense of individual responsibility when the government assumes control over more and more areas of life? When a difficult situation prompts us not to planning and effort but to a cry for "government aid"?

A group of young people studied the Lord's Prayer one day. They broke up into work groups, each one with a petition from the Lord's Prayer. Their assignment was to compose a liturgy of specific petitions under each of the seven petitions of the Lord's Prayer. At the end of the session there was a prayer service in the sanctuary. The pastor prayed each petition; the young people responded with the specific petitions which they had prepared. This is the prayer they offered under the Fourth Petition:

Pastor: "Give us this day our daily bread."

Youth: "Dear God, please help the government see that everybody gets all the things they need."[103.]

This is idolatry. A benevolent government taking over the chores of the Heavenly Father. The apotheosis of the State is not ushered in with 60-cubit idols and military parades, but with pumpkins and treats.

Once we release to the government the responsibility for alleviating human needs, we also relinquish the authority for determining human needs. The tax dollar which today goes for food stamps in Appalachia, in another day, under the aegis of a different regime, may go to sterilize 'unproductive' members of society. Even today our freedom to minister to those in need is circumscribed considerably. As church members, we may want to pour our personal resources into seminary education in our denomination, or to support a half-way house for drug addicts. But that kind of alternative is not altogether left open to us. Whether we like it or not, we are forced to support urban renewal, poverty programs, and a host of other programs. The intrusion of the government into the field of social welfare robs a citizen of his freedom to support those causes which God may especially lay on his heart; to the extent that his money is forcibly diverted to other projects through taxation, he is less able to support projects of his own choosing. Again the issue is, freedom versus coercion.

And it is precisely here that the deepest damage is done. For we have focused our whole attention on the need of the poor or 'disadvantaged.' We have utterly neglected the need of the man with something to give. The need to learn and practice compassion is perhaps less urgent, but by the same token more profound.

Lazarus was poor, but he ended up in Abraham's bosom; the rich man was selfish, and he ended up in torment. Which of the two men had the greater 'need,' seen at long range?[104.] A welfare program supported by compulsory taxes may alleviate Lazarus' need. But it goes flat against both the rights and the needs of the rich man.

Far from complementing the Christian Gospel, government welfare programs can positively hinder it. Through taxation they force upon us a materialistic concept of man. We are compelled to pour our resources into ever greater and greater programs to alleviate material want. Resources which we might want to channel to other areas — missionary work, colleges, cultural centers — are siphoned off by a government which implicitly proclaims the satisfaction of material wants as the highest good.

The job of alleviating real human want, at least for its own members, is a privilege which the church should not readily surrender to a secular government. The voluntary charity and privately supported welfare programs may not move as quickly as government programs. But this passion for hurrying up the process can involve us in an outright repudiation of Christian teaching. *For the opportunity to choose or reject the Christian Faith lies at the very heart of the Gospel.* Slow and frustrating it may often be, but as a Christian one can never sidestep this basic tenet of free choice. Any time we try to elicit a Christian response by force, we are substituting the way of tyranny for the way of Jesus.

The hurry-up process is tempting. Forcing people to be good involves fewer problems and fewer frustrations than the slow, patient way of Jesus. But perhaps, as Dorothy Sayers has put it, there is a reason for it — a reason which God Himself had to endure...

Hard it is, very hard,
To travel up the slow and stony road
To Calvary, to redeem mankind; far better

To make but one resplendent miracle,
Lean through the cloud, lift the right hand of power
And with a sudden lightning smite the world perfect!
Yet this was not God's way, who had the power,
But set it by, choosing the cross, the thorn,
The sorrowful wounds. Something there is, perhaps,
That power destroys in passing, something supreme,
To whose great value in the eyes of God
That cross, that thorn, and those five wounds
    bear witness.[105.]

Have the massive government attempts of the last forty years to 'smite the world perfect' brought us any closer to the Kingdom of God? Or have they, piecemeal, contributed to the destruction of that something supreme, that Jesus died rather than violate?

When a government welfare program is argued from the standpoint of charity, humanitarianism, helpfulness toward the unfortunate, a Christian, precisely because of his Christian beliefs, may well have to oppose it flatly. Where this kind of need exists, it is a job for the Christian himself, and those who share his concern.

If the job is too big for them, then they will simply have to work and pray harder. And bend their efforts to meet the corrolary need: *persuading* others to join in. But never submit to the temptation to *force* them. For a man has the right to dispose of his property according to his own conscience, not according to ours, or the majority's. His answerability is to God, not society, if he is selfish.

Having said this much, we recognize that "Christian charity" is not the only rationale for government welfare programs, though it is surely that which social theologians most often put forward. A purely pragmatic case might be argued for government welfare projects, showing how they would contribute to peace and order, preservation of freedom, protection of the citizenry, and therefore would merit support from the general populace.

Paradoxically, a Christian is more free to support a secular welfare program when it is presented on pragmatic grounds, than when it is presented as an extension of the Christian Faith. For when the argument is merely pragmatic, it does not involve one in an attempt to implement the Christian Faith by means of coercion.

The penchant for undue moralizing in political affairs is not so much a Christian, as it is an American trait, as John Erskin once pointed out in addressing a Phi Beta Kappa chapter: "We Americans are too much inclined to make a moral issue of an economic or social question, because it seems ignoble to admit it as simply a question of intelligence."[106.]

Where a government welfare program can be shown to make good political and social sense, a Christian citizen may decide to give it his support. Our concern has been to call into question a too simplistic identification of secular welfare programs with the Christian Gospel.

As Christians, our concern is that our behavior as citizens remain consistent with our Christian beliefs. Insofar as we join in trying to force the structures of society into a "Christian" mold, we cut the nerve of the Gospel. A charismatic approach to social action recognizes that apart from a free response of faith, the Gospel does not function.

Over the long run, the greatest service which the church can perform in and for the world is to *be* that household of faith which, by its example, demonstrates a better way of life.

Through His people — through communities of Christians drawn together under the leading of the Holy Spirit

—the Lord surely does stretch out His hand to help and to heal some of the hurts of the world, as He Himself did, while upon earth. But through these communities the world receives more than a helping hand. It receives the example of a people who have learned to deal with the social issues of life in a deeply effective way.

Where the Christian community becomes the kind of caring fellowship that captures the attention of the world, new possibilities for reaching the world will begin to open up. Present day stereotypes will give way to a truly biblical evangelism.

"You can't preach the Gospel to a hungry man. The disadvantaged, the alienated, the down-trodden will not listen to our preaching until we first minister to their physical, social, economic, and political needs." So goes the stereotype.

A false dichotomy sometimes intrudes at this juncture. "Evangelism" is pitted against "social action." In fact, however, evangelism is itself a form of social action. Even though its goals are not limited to life in this world, it nevertheless does offer practical help for the betterment of life in this world. The fact that the kind of help it offers is primarily spiritual rather than material does not make the help any the less real, necessary, or effectual precisely for life in this world. Unless we surrender entirely to a materialistic concept of life, we will recognize that the practical betterment of life in this world depends on spiritual as well as material factors. The contrast is thus not between evangelism and social action, but rather between spiritual and material welfare. Which should have the priority?

A charismatic approach to social issues would not take a dogmatic stand on one side or the other. It would allow for the possibility that the stereotype cited above could represent the leading of the Holy Spirit in given situations. But it would not agree that this is necessarily, or even normally, the case.

Two simple facts stand in coordinate relation to one another in the New Testament: 1) In the culture of that day there existed no dearth of 'problems': famine, starvation, political oppression, repressive institutions, poverty. 2) The primary concern evidenced by the primitive Christian community, living in that culture, was to *spread the Good News*. Ministering to material needs, even in the case of fellow believers, and much more so in the case of the general culture, assumed a decidedly derivative and secondary role.

This was not an either/or proposition,[107] but a case of this primarily/that secondarily.[108] This priority arrangement, as the normal order of things, is rooted in the anthropological stance of the New Testament, which views the state of a man's soul and spirit as more critical to his real welfare than his immediate material circumstances. "Therefore I tell you, do not be anxious about your life, what you shall eat, nor about your body, what you shall put on. For life is more than food, and the body more than clothing."[109]

The preaching of the Good News is the first order of business of the church, not because she is introverted and unconcerned, but precisely because she has a radical outgoing concern for all men who come within reach of her ministry. Those who set aside this priority arrangement do not take man's real condition seriously. His material needs may be urgent; his spiritual need is critical and therefore of first importance.

This does not mean that one must literally preach a sermon to a man before ever he lifts a finger to offer material help of any kind. The priority is a priority of *concern*, not necessarily of actual ministry.

While it recognizes the priority of ministering to a

man's spiritual need, a charismatic approach seeks to unite evangelism and social action in its ministry to each person. With each encounter there is evangelism, and also appropriate social action.

If an encounter does not permit of an evangelistic thrust, it must be questioned. This is a control-principle necessitated by the priority we assign to evangelism. If we cannot sound the evangelistic note relatively toward the beginning of the operation, then we had better re-check our signals.

With each person we reach, there must be this dual emphasis. Which means that the opposite question must also be posed: "Are we helping this person in the practical needs and issues of his everyday life?" A church which neglects to minister to people's material and practical needs can too easily end up as little more than a Bible study group; or, worse, a social club.

On the other hand, if we make material help our primary concern, and simply lock arms with the good humanists, we may help to provide people with a measure of temporary relief, but we will thereby have communicated to them something about the relative importance of the Gospel, which no amount of teaching will erase. The church gives priority to the Gospel because it wants to give the world its *best,* rather than a poor second-best. It does not matter that the world in its darkness puts a higher initial valuation on the second-best; if the church dances to the world's tune she will never attract anything but "rice Christians." It is the church's mission to present the Good News of salvation in Christ as the greatest piece of social action to ever hit the planet.

If a man were a doctor, and a killer epidemic were spreading through the community, and in his office he had a medicine which could stem the tide of the epidemic — the *only* medicine which could cure that disease —

then the best thing which he could do for the community, the very best thing, would be to get that medicine to the people. There might be a lot of other "good things" that he could do in the community. They need some business and professional people active in the Chamber of Commerce, the PTA, service clubs. They're having a civic beautification drive next month, and need some people to help organize it. They need managers and sponsors for Little League; he could do that. He could do any or all of these things, and it would be of some help to some people.

But if a killer disease were spreading through the community, and he had the medicine and skill to cure it, then all these other things would become, quite literally, 'little league.' Nothing wrong with them at all. They just are not the thing he can afford to spend his time on when people are dying every day for lack of the medicine which he alone could be giving them.

The church today is something like this doctor. It is being pressured into a lot of little league activities, which may be worthwhile enough in themselves, but which divert our attention and energy from the one thing which the world most needs from us, and which we alone are able to give — the Good News of salvation, as a lived experience.

These little league activities, as we have seen, generally get lumped together under the label of 'social action,' by which one means actions to better man's social, economic, or political situation. "God is concerned about all of man's needs and problems," so goes the reasoning, "and therefore the church must minister to human need wherever it turns up." In support of this, some such text as the parable of the Good Samaritan is usually cited. It is probably the *locus classicus* for those who argue the priority of man's material needs. It merits some analysis.

Consider, first, the broad, and then the immediate,

context for the parable of the Good Samaritan. It is found in Luke 10. The chapter begins with Jesus' sending out of the 70 disciples. After an eminently effective mission (even the demons were subject to them), they return. "In that same hour Jesus rejoiced in the Holy Spirit and said, 'I thank Thee, Father, Lord of heaven and earth, that Thou hast hidden these things from the wise and understanding and revealed them to babes.'"[110.] Even allowing for Jesus' mild rebuke ("Nevertheless, do not rejoice in this, that the spirits are subject to you; but rejoice that your names are written in heaven."), it is evident that He heartily endorses the kind of ministry that they have carried out for Him — a ministry of preaching and miracle-working. The emphasis and priority is clear-cut. This forms the prelude to the parable of the Good Samaritan.

Now comes the lead-up to the famous story. In typical rabbinic give-and-take style, Jesus and an ecclesiastical lawyer establish the essential criteria for obtaining eternal life: love of God, and love of neighbor. "But the lawyer, *desiring to justify himself,* said to Jesus, 'And who is my neighbor?'"[111.] How easily we skim over those four words, "desiring to justify himself." Yet they are absolutely critical to the evangelist's understanding of the incident. The parable is specifically directed to one *who wished to justify himself* — a task which Christian theology understands to be humanly impossible. Unless we get a sense of the Impossible which pervades this parable, we are bound to miss its significance.

If you went to a John Birch Society meeting, and heard someone extolling Angela Davis in heroine terms, you'd have something of the emotional flavor of Jesus' story of the Good Samaritan. It was calculated to produce a startled "Impossible!" from those who heard it — pious Jews who, for good, sound, orthodox, religious reasons, looked down on the Samaritans as scum. We've lost the emotional climate and so we've lost most of the meaning.

We make it out to be a touching story of human compassion, calculated to urge us on to a few more neighborly tries. But this is precisely what Jesus did *not* want. What did He want?

The sequel provides the commentary: The story of Martha and Mary, with which the chapter ends. Hectic activity is not the suitable follow-up to the parable of the Good Samaritan, but rather a seeking after Jesus, a willingness to sit at His feet and be taught. Just because the story of the Good Samaritan is so utterly impossible, from a human point-of-view, we must seek the One who specializes in the impossible, must absorb the Spirit of Him who is devoid of prejudice and hang-ups of all kinds. *And this is the essential, primary need of the people whom we meet in the world.*

It is no happenstance that this parable is set between the sending out of the 70, and the incident in the house of Martha and Mary. In both of these real-life situations, we see the kind of priority which Jesus and His disciples follow as they minister in the world. The parable, by contrast, presents a hypothetical situation specifically directed to a man whose concern was not for people, but for his own justification. The context thus serves as a frame, to keep a masterpiece of Jesus from curling and cracking beyond recognition. Apart from the preaching and the teaching of the Gospel, our efforts to play the Good Samaritan will degenerate into a self-justifying Pharisaism.

A concern for the priority of evangelism, as over against a ministry which provides material welfare as a first order of business, thus rests upon two bases of understanding: 1) Man's most critical need is for the Good News of Salvation, a saving relationship with Jesus Christ; 2) Unless this priority is observed, our efforts to help others will be little more than an exercise in self-justification.

The impact of the church upon the world depends upon

the quality of life which is lived in the household of faith. Where this is authentic, the world can look in and see 'how they love one another.' The Gospel will gain a credibility in the midst of an age of jaundiced skepticism. And some of these will enter into the Christian community. They will become part of this household of faith, where "evangelism" and "social action" function as an everyday expression of life.

Chapter Eight
THE SERVANT CHURCH

The New Testament sets down no neat dogmatic definition of the church's role in the social structure. What we find are allusions, epigrams, analogies, incidents, even meaningful silences which, when pieced together, form a kind of mosaic. They give us an impression, a sense of outline, but no detailed description. In the wisdom of God, that was left to the leading of the Holy Spirit, as the church lived out her witness in concrete historical moments.

We live in an historical moment when the church not only needs the guidance of the Holy Spirit in specific situations (this is ever so), but particularly needs a fresh impression of the mosaic. Unless we recognize the general outline of God's purpose for the church in the system of this world, specific attempts at social action are likely to fly wide of the mark.

What understanding of the church's role in society is generally current today? Many churchmen have focused with a kind of myopic rapture upon one piece of the mosaic, the "servant" motif. The "Servant Church" has graduated to the status of a theological slogan. Briefly stated, it is this: The church, like Jesus, is cast in the role of servant. The world cries out in need, and the church steps in to serve that need.

The root of the concept is found in the "servant" passages of Isaiah, where the Messiah is pictured as servant. But in applying the concept to the church's program of social action, a not-so-subtle mutation sets in. In Isaiah, the "servant" is quite unambiguously the servant *of the Lord.* He serves the Lord, fulfilling His purpose, most especially His purposes of redemption: "By his knowledge shall the righteous one, my servant, make many to be accounted righteous; and he shall bear their iniquities."[112.]

But in the parlance of contemporary social theology, the "Servant Church" becomes the servant of the world. The practical conclusion to which this leads, in practice if not in theory, is that the church now takes its cues from the world. Casting herself in the role of servant, the church, perhaps unthinkingly, has cast the world in the role of master.

This comes out in down-to-earth situations. A theologian, for instance, addresses a church convention and says that "whereas God has written the constitution for the church, the world writes the agenda!"[113.] Even as I was preparing this material, I attended a church service where a layman spoke, and used this identical phrase: "We have to take the world's agenda as our own!" God may have laid down some broad guidelines, but the church must look to the world for her day-to-day instructions.

Church members are told that one of the criteria for a program of social action is that those in need must themselves be left to determine how the money will be spent.[114.] Again, the church must serve according to the will and determination of the world. The servant-master roles could hardly be delineated more explicitly.

Surely there is a large element of truth in the "Servant Church" motif (the nature of heresy is not the importation of alien falsehood, but the perverting of essential truth).

The church *is* sent into the world to serve—sent by the Lord. But that is quite another thing from being called *by the world* to serve the world.

The list of needs which the world sets for itself may be quite different than the priorities which God sets for it. The church serves the world only at those places and in those ways and toward those ends which God may determine.

The servanthood of the church is as over-against the Lordship of Christ. Her serving of the world is, in a formal sense, incidental. Like a trustworthy servant, she is ready to serve wherever her Lord may assign her. If it be in the world, well and good. If another assignment were made, if the church were called out of or away from the world,[115.] that would be all right too. A new sphere of service, but the same Lord. The servant role would not be essentially changed.

The servanthood of the church, separated from the absolute Lordship of Christ, cuts the church adrift on a tossing sea of human need without compass, map, or rudder. Direction for the Servant Church can as little be found by inquiring of the world, as a mariner might guide his ship by taking a fix on the passing waves. The true Servant Church must continually check her position in relation to the timeless question: "Lord, what would *You* have me to do?" A charismatic approach to social issues begins by asking this primary question.

As we have seen, the Servant Church is called by its Master to be a 'light,' a community which offers an alternative to the darkness in the world. It serves the world not merely by what it does, but—more essentially—by what it *is*. The most essential service which the church offers to the world is that of *example*. "Do good to all men, *and especially to those who are of the household of faith*."[116.]

At first glance, the Apostle's word might appear to be self-serving. Wouldn't it be more "Christian" to give first to others? In a given instance, perhaps. But not as a general rule, and not over the long haul. "Give a man a fish and he'll be hungry tomorrow. Teach a man to fish and he'll feed his whole family."

God does not mean for the church to cure all the ills or solve all the problems of the world, but rather to let the world know where help and healing can be found. While we may be called on to share our riches with others, it is equally, and perhaps more important, that we reveal their own riches to them.

Calvary Chapel, a center for the "Jesus Movement" in Costa Mesa, California, opened up a house for dropouts and dope addicts in 1967. They saw some spectacular changes in the lives of young people. These people moved into the community of faith. In turn, they began to go out and draw in other young people. Something was happening: The light was shining in the darkness!

People from other communities began to drop by. "What's happening?" they wanted to know. "How can we get something like this going?" Chuck Smith, the pastor of the church, went at it this way: When they found a nucleus of people who wanted to start up this kind of a ministry, they passed on all the know-how they had, and they paid the first month's rent on a house. After that, the new house was on its own, trusting the Lord, as Calvary Chapel itself had had to do. This *example* of one caring community has multiplied itself more than 100 times over, with houses springing up all along the West Coast, and as far east as Denver, Colorado.[117.]

Jesus recognized the explosive potential in the example of a household of faith, knit together in love. Our human response would lead us to conclude that the love which we show directly to the world would be our most powerful testimony. On occasion this might be so, and the Holy Spirit might so lead. But as a general rule, Jesus knew that it was otherwise. "By *this* will all men know that you are my disciples, if you have love *for one another.*"[118.]

The world is said to have looked on the early church, and exclaimed, "Behold, how they love one another!" This was the kind of thing that drew them irresistibly not only to, but into, the Christian community. Paradoxically, the love which the church shows to her own will, in the long run, become a greater blessing to the world than the love which she may manifest directly to the world. It is rooted in the eschatological vision and purpose. God wants to draw men into the household of faith, and the love which the believers show toward one another is part of that which attracts and draws. Paul, at one point, frankly admits that he wants to stir outsiders up to jealousy, in order to bring them in.[119.]

Jim Cavnar, speaking on "Evangelism and Social Action" at a National Leaders' Conference of the Catholic Charismatic Renewal, in Ann Arbor, Michigan, struck the fundamental note of New Testament social thought when he said, "Building the Body of Christ *is itself a service to the world.*" One might go a step further, and say that building up the Body of Christ is *the* service, *par excellence,* which the church offers to the world.

It is at this point that we begin to break new ground in our consideration of social action. For it leads us beyond the false dichotomy which has polarized discussion about social issues.

"In the last fifty years theological liberals have tended to stress social issues to the exclusion of the preaching of the Gospel to individuals, whereas theological conservatives have done the reverse."[120.] This is a fairly typical statement of the dichotomy which one continually encounters in any serious discussion of social theology. A non-evangelical social activism is pitted against a highly individualistic evangelicalism. In theory, one is often told, "we must have both." In practice, the dichotomy proves more formidable; lines are drawn, and camps are set up in essential opposition to one another.

Neither alternative, nor any makeshift compromise between them, grasps the nettle of New Testament social thought. The New Testament response to social ills is neither the reform of secular institutions, nor individualistic piety, but a new social organism, the Body of Christ, living out her life and mission in the midst of the world.

Contemporary social theology has failed to grasp the radical nature of the Gospel, as it applies to social issues. It has taken the imperatives of the Gospel as though they were handed down from Mt. Sinai, rather than Calvary; as law rather than Gospel. It seeks to apply New Testament principles indiscriminately to society at large, whereas Jesus and the Apostles carefully circumscribed their admonitions to the household of faith. And for a very good reason.

The imperatives of the Gospel are not simple human possibilities. The Gospel describes a quality and style of life which is impossible, humanly speaking. By his own effort, man can neither attain nor maintain that life which the Gospel sets forth. The Gospel can only be lived by the power of the Holy Spirit. To apply the standard of the Gospel to society at large lays upon society an intolerable burden, for the enabling factor (the Holy Spirit) is missing. It is like admonishing a crab apple tree to begin producing grapes.

The church which seeks to change the structures of society so that they will reflect, let us say, the spirit of love described by St. Paul in I Corinthians 13, has set for itself an impossible task. Any attempt to do so can only result in an endless proliferation of legal restraints and compulsions.

The world does not understand the Gospel, indeed cannot. It will always translate the Gospel into a new law, because law is the only language which is understood in society at large. The Gospel can be understood and lived only in a community indwelt by the Holy Spirit.

The New Testament leaves us in no doubt as to where the Holy Spirit dwells. He does not dwell in society at large, nor in any of the structures of society. "The world *cannot receive Him,* because it does not know Him."[121.] The Holy Spirit indwells the church, the household of faith. Only there does the Gospel become a possibility. To attempt to conform any other community to the Gospel is a folly, a presumption, and an arrogant imposition.

The world may observe some of the things which the Spirit-filled church does, and even approve. But what it sees will have limited application in the structures of society. Because that which makes it work in the church is not know-how or can-do, but the presence and power of the Holy Spirit. Apart from this x-factor, the equation does not add up. Without the Holy Spirit, the visible structures and techniques which the church employs produce at best a mixed result.

The church which attempts to merchandise its life values to the structures of society is guilty of gross misrepresentation. It purports to offer a vehicle for bringing society to a higher level of justice and righteousness, but it cannot provide the motive power. We may attempt to baptize the structures of society all we please. The Spirit continues to blow where He will. He continues to dwell in the only place He ever said that He would dwell, the church.

The church which arrogates to itself the task of reforming society, by that very inclination betrays the atrophy of its faith and life. It has ceased to depend upon God for all it says and does. It no longer has the mind of Christ, who said, "I can do nothing of myself, but only what I see the Father do."[122.] It is filled with a sense of what it can *do,* of strength and capability. It has come to rely upon worldly judgment, worldly capability, worldly resources. It has the form of the Christian religion, but not its power. And so it does not perceive any critical difference between the church and the institutions of society. Because it has learned to espouse a form of righteousness with no recourse to any other power than the power of its own will and good intention, it presumes that the world can and ought to do the same. And so it casts itself in the role of "prophet," proclaiming to the world a better way of life, a higher standard of righteousness. As though that were what the world needed; as though the structures of society had within themselves the power to put into effect the implications of the Gospel. As though the Cross and the Open Tomb and Pentecost had never or need never have happened.

The church which lives in the power and plenitude of the Spirit carries within its bosom a deep sense of dependence upon God. "Apart from me you can do nothing."[123.] It has been awakened to a sense of powerlessness – and yet, through Christ it can do all things. It is not a lawgiver or prophet of righteousness to society, but a *witness* – a witness of what Christ is and does when He dwells among His people. The Spirit-filled church is not concerned to lecture the world, but rather to itself become, through the working of the Holy Spirit, that example to the world of a community of people whom Christ has transformed.

This, then, is where the servanthood of the church begins: She becomes the Body of Christ; she becomes the 'place' where the truth and power of God break through into the world. Until that Body is formed and functioning, the 'Servant Church' remains a pious theological abstraction.

Jesus entered into His servanthood at a very precise moment in time: When He became incarnate, when He was 'found in human form.'[124.] Except He humbled Himself and took on a body, He could not become the Servant of the Lord.

As individuals, our servanthood begins when we humble ourselves to become a part of the Body of Christ. Not in some spiritual or abstract sense, but in concrete, visible reality. We join ourselves to a community of fellow Christians. We become as committed to that body of believers as to the Lord; more exactly, our commitment to the community *is* our commitment to the Lord.

This may not seem as 'spiritual' as a commitment to the Lord. That is the gnostic heresy of our day. The gnostics in the early church taught a 'spiritual gospel.' It was too 'unspiritual' to think of Jesus literally committed to a body of flesh. So they explained away the Incarnation: It was a spiritual truth, but not a physical reality. Modern-day gnostics do the same thing with the church, which is the Body of Christ. "You do not need to be joined to the church; the important thing is that you have a spiritual relationship with Christ." It sounds spiritual, but it has a fatal flaw: It is not the way which God has arranged for us to be joined to Christ. We are joined to Christ by being baptized into His Body.[125.] That is the practical meaning and outcome of the Incarnation. The Body of Christ, a visible community of believers indwelt by the Holy Spirit and knit together in love, is God's answer to gnostics in every age.

A charismatic approach to social issues, then, sees the building up of the Body of Christ as a first order of business. This has a twofold effect on the world. Its primary effect is a demonstration to the world of an alternative life-style – a new social organism *in* the world, but not *of* the world. Some will be drawn by this example themselves to be joined to this body of believers, which is God's ultimate purpose.

A secondary effect will be a dealing with concrete needs and issues which the Holy Spirit sets before a given community of believers. As we have noted, throughout the charismatic movement there is an increasing concern with social issues. The stereotype of a highly individualistic evangelicalism, which sees no further than one's "decision for Christ" fails to describe what is emerging in the charismatic movement.

The pioneering work of David Wilkerson with drug addicts has been picked up and applied by numerous charismatic groups. The Episcopal Church of the Redeemer, in Houston, Texas, has gained national attention with its programs of social action.

St. John's Lutheran Church in Massapequa, New York made an organized and frustrating attempt to "help" an inner-city church in the Bronx, a more-or-less typical social action project.

"It fizzled," said John Hove, pastor of the suburban church. "They have learned to be suspicious of one-shot heroics."

Some time later, a single individual from the Massapequa congregation felt a leading to go down to the Bronx community on Saturdays, contacting young people on a one-to-one basis. Others began to join him. They worked with the young people and their families. And in the inner-city community the word went out: "Don't bother these people. They really care."[126.]

A prayer group in a rural Minnesota town sparked the first person-to-person outreach to nearby Indian families which that community had witnessed in living memory. And this at precisely the time when the Indians had let it be known that if the activist American Indian Movement showed up in *their* territory, they would be met with leveled rifles.[127.]

Without organization or fanfare, these kind of things are happening. A distinctive style of servanthood is emerging in the charismatic movement. In a quiet way, charismatics are beginning to do the kind of thing that social activists have been calling for.

Yet it is clear that charismatics are not "social activists," in the classic sense. Wherein lies the difference? It can be seen in three specific regards: A charismatic approach to social issues is different as regards its *motivation*, as regards its *operation*, and as regards its ultimate *purpose.*

The key word in the lexicon of social activism is *justice.* We are urged to adopt an agenda of causes which promises to correct injustice, and insure 'rights.' While people are to be the alleged beneficiaries of these rights, the spear-tip of zeal is directed primarily toward institutions — social, political, religious. It's the *system* that's wrong. We must change the structures of society, in order to help those who are being denied simple justice.

In the equations of classic social activism, people become an object of concern, rather than the subject of a personal encounter. The activist approach is thus essentially paternalistic. It caused one observer of the inner-city scene to remark, "The liberal, activist churches have generally been less successful in reaching the people of the inner-city than the Pentecostal store-front operations. The activists came in as benefactors, while the Pentecostals came in as brothers."[128.]

In the charismatic movement, the rhetoric of justice and rights has occupied a less prominent position. More often one hears words like 'call,' 'leading,' 'obedience.' The motivation for a particular work comes in response to what is believed to be specific divine initiative.

Traditional social activism has a hard time with this kind of thing. It has been schooled to reason from abstraction to application; to move from a general principle (such as 'justice') to a specific conclusion (such as boycotting table grapes) by what is believed to be a process of simple rational deduction. For one trained to think in this way, the charismatic's sometimes too-breezy "The Lord told me..." comes across as maddeningly smug.

In the charismatic movement, however, "The Lord told me..." is no light phrase. It is the motivation behind a growing number of works of social concern. Where the conviction is born that God has spoken, charismatics back up their conviction with a measure of commitment and sacrifice which is difficult to dispute. When white upper-middle-class professional people sell their homes and move into a minority ghetto—and stay there, with a quiet ministry of love and concern—one begins to think that perhaps, after all, the Lord *did* tell them....

A charismatic approach to social action does not set out to reform society. Its concern is to remain responsive and obedient to the Lord. The good that charismatics may do in the world is a by-product of their obedience to the Lord. The church qualifies as 'servant' not in that it serves the world where it thinks the world might be well served, or where the world wants to be served, but in that it obeys its Master, serving in that place which He has pointed out. This is the understanding of servanthood which characteristically motivates works of social action in the charismatic movement.

Linked to a growing social concern in the charismatic

movement has been a strong tendency toward *community.* Since the late 1960's, it has become clear that the goal of the renewal goes beyond the transformation of the individual. The *Body* must be transformed and become a witness. In a variety of ways, charismatics are drawing together to share their lives on more than a Sunday-morning basis.

Words like 'household,' 'extended family,' 'Christian community' are heard with increasing frequency in charismatic gatherings, where ten years ago one would more likely have heard about 'tongues,' 'prophecy,' 'healing,' 'baptism with the Holy Spirit.' Not that these have dropped out of the picture; the frame has been enlarged. The renewal of personal spiritual life has opened the door to a new dimension of corporate Christian experience.

These communities serve as a base for works of social concern. The traditional approach to social action has been to mobilize people around a cause. In the charismatic movement a different kind of operation is emerging. The primary orientation in the charismatic movement is not toward a cause, but toward community. Where charismatics take up a work of social concern, it is as an expression of a primary commitment to community. Social action operates as a function or expression of the life of the community.

What touches the world, therefore, is more than a helping hand. It is a whole body, a community of believers, a *life.* This has a distinctive effect on the style of social action. The emphasis is not merely on meeting a need, but, more fundamentally, on meeting a person.

Most forms of community life involve a certain commitment of material possessions to the community. The inevitable result of this is to deepen the level of personal relationships within the community (sometimes painfully so!). You cannot enter into an extended sharing of possessions without at the same time sharing more deeply your life together.

The person who comes forth from a community, therefore, tends to have a somewhat different attitude toward the material needs of life. He is less prone to superficial guilt reactions when presented with cases of material want. Material possessions have begun to assume a less dominant position in his own life, while personal relationships have begun to take on greater meaning.

When he is called to help minister to some need, he is not satisfied to look only at the outstretched hand. He wants to look into the face and eyes. He wants also to minister to that deeper need — *that need to be known, to be seen as a person, to be recognized and received in love.* The social action which is coming out of charismatic Christian communities tends to talk less in terms of "problems" and "issues," more in terms of people — and people not as an abstract mass-in-need, but in terms of specific individuals whom one comes to know, appreciate, and love.

A vicar's wife in Northern Ireland saw the charismatic movement beginning to have this kind of effect in the midst of the political and social turmoil of that country. "We don't make much headway," she said, "but the one hopeful sign is that in this Pentecostal movement we are experiencing a measure of unity."[129.]

A charismatic approach to social action thus operates as an outgrowth of life-in-community. Its focus is not merely on a need or a problem, but on persons. The enrichment of personal relationships, which has been fostered in the community of believers, carries over into the works of social concern to which the Lord calls the community.

Finally, a charismatic approach to social action differs

from a traditional attitude toward social action in terms of its ultimate purpose. Traditional social action looks for the renewal of society, through a perfecting of its institutions. By means of just laws, equitable economic programs, humane and responsive political structures, one expects to see God's purpose being accomplished in the world. The focus is primarily upon program and structure—change these, and society will be renewed.

A charismatic approach to social action also looks for the renewal of society. But it does not expect this to come about simply through reforming the structures. New structures by themselves tend to exchange one set of problems for another—oust the king, and usher in the Robespierre. More than new structures, the world needs new *people.*

Evangelicals have traditionally said, "Renew the person, and (by a simple process of extension) society will be renewed." But the issue goes deeper than that. Social action is more than something which renewed people do. Social action is itself a part of the process by which renewal is effected.

On the one hand, therefore, a charismatic approach to social action steers clear of the naive hope that a reorganized society will be a renewed society. But, on the other hand, it also recognizes that the renewal which God envisions does not end simply with so many renewed charismatic individuals living charitable, law-abiding lives.

At an international charismatic conference at Nottingham University in England, Presbyterian leader Tom Smails made the point that the charismatic renewal must move beyond the level of individual transformation. "The world has all kinds of gifted individuals," he said, *but the world doesn't know how to live together.*"[130.]

The purpose of God is to raise up in the world a renewed

community, which begins even now to manifest the power and glory of the age to come. The Christian community is meant to be, for the world, a Prevue of Coming Attractions. Like the Prevues at the local cinema, it gives out enough hints and promises to capture the viewer's imagination, and to galvanize his will to the point where he says, "I *must* take that one in!"

The Prevue is not a simulation of the real thing; it is a fragment of the real thing. It is taken from the real film, but it is not the whole show, only a part. The Holy Spirit, as the Divine Editor, selects works of social action which demonstrate some aspect of the Kingdom. Like the scenes in the Prevue, these works, regarded as a whole, are neither comprehensive nor connected. They are, rather, suggestive, illuminative, provocative, gripping, engaging. Their purpose is not to build the Kingdom, but to announce – not merely in words, but in live action – the Kingdom which the Lord has already built, and which is coming to town for a long-term engagement. Tickets now on sale at the box office.

"The true Christian community," Arthur Richter points out, "has always been relatively small. We know now that there has never really been anything approaching a 'Christian nation,' and likely such a thing was never intended by God.

"The Christian community has no leverage of worldly power at its disposal. It can never pressure or compel the society at large. It can only live and serve in the midst of that society. As a concrete illustration of a new way of life, it can awaken in other men a new hope.

"It matters not whether great goals are reached by the Christian community. The important thing is that the creative impulse is given."[131.]

A charismatic approach to social action thus will not content itself to build its programs upon a shaky, makeshift foundation of human plans and conceptions. It 'looks for a city which has foundations, whose builder and maker is God.'[132.] On the one hand, it knows that any work of social action, seen by itself, will be fragmentary, fleeting, of small consequence. Yet, on the other hand, it knows that every work initiated by the Spirit has a power and potential beyond any earthly reckoning, because it participates in the reality of the Kingdom.

"The tides of the Spirit rise higher and higher," writes Erwin Prange, out of his experience as a charismatic Lutheran pastor serving in the inner-city. "Charismatics do not return to their previous level. In the ten years that I have been a part of the spiritual renewal, the renewal itself has changed. God is always doing a new thing and is constantly shaping a new creation out of the old. God Himself does not change, but He is constantly changing His creatures."[133.]

God's final answer to the problems of society is the establishment of His own society. Peace and justice will finally come upon the earth when the Prince of Peace has taken up His scepter, when the "kingdom of this world has become the kingdom of our Lord and of His Christ, and he shall reign for ever and ever."[134.] In the meantime, people made alive and joined together by His Spirit into vital Christian communities, will move in the midst of the world as God's Great Advertisement, so that the world can see and feel and be touched by the reality of His Kingdom.

NOTES

1. Arndt and Gingrich. *A Greek-English Lexicon of the New Testament and other early Christian Literature,* p. 887. University of Chicago Press, 1957.

2. McDonnell, Kilian. *Catholic Pentecostalism: Problems in Evaluation,* p. 19. Dove Publications, Pecos, New Mexico.

3. Van Dusen, Henry P. *Spirit, Son, and Father,* pp. 18-19. Charles Scribner's Sons, New York, 1958.

4. Private information.

5. Psalm 127:1

6. Cavnar, Jim. Talk given to a consultation of leaders in the Lutheran Charismatic Renewal, Ann Arbor, Michigan, October 11, 1973.

7. McDonnell, *op. cit.,* p. 20.

8. Wilkerson, Ralph. In conversation, at a conference in Anaheim, California, August 18, 1973.

9. Galatians 3:1, 3

10. Private information.

11. Bradley, Ian. "'Saints' Against Sin," *Christianity Today,* June 8, 1973, pp. 15-16.

12. Vanderkooi, Garret. "Evolution As A Scientific Theory," *Christianity Today,* May 7, 1971, p. 741.

13. Burnham, James. *Suicide of the West,* pp. 31-32. The John Day Company, New York, 1964.

14. John 5:19

15. Wilkerson, David. Spoken at a youth rally at Melodyland, Anaheim, California.

16. Pulkingham, Graham, In a lecture at an International Charismatic Conference, Nottingham University, England, July 13, 1973.

17. Song of Solomon 1:4

18. Prange, Erwin. *The Gift Is Already Yours*, p. 113. Logos International, Plainfield, N.J., 1973. Italics added.

19. Acts 12:6-12

20. Numbers 14:6-9

21. Numbers 14:44, 45

22. Acts 16:6-10

23. Kallas, James. *The Satanward View*, p. 32. The Westminster Press, Philadelphia, Pa., 1956.

24. Kelsey, Morton. "Angels, Demons, and Other Spiritual Entities." Unpublished manuscript, pp. 1-2. The substance of this monograph is included in Kelsey's Book, *Encounter With God, A Theology of Christian Experience,* Bethany Fellowship, 1972.

25. White, Victor, O. P. *God and the Unconscious,* pp. 192ff. The World Publishing Company (Meridian Books), Cleveland, Ohio, 1961.

26. Kelsey, Morton, *op. cit.,* p. 2

27. Galatians 6:10a

28. von Campenhausen, Hans. *Tradition and Life in the Early Church,* pp. 141, 143, 147, 154. Fortress Press, Philadelphia, Pa., 1968.

29. I Timothy 2:1-4

30. Luke 16:25, 18:24

31. Mark 14:7-9

32. Colossians 2:15

33. 2 Corinthians 10:4

34. I John 5:19

35. James 1:20

36. Private information.

37. Private correspondence.

38. Prince, Derek. *Shaping History Through Prayer and Fasting,* pp. 138-147. Fleming H. Revell Company, Old Tappan, New Jersey, 1973.

39. See Colossians 2:15

40. Hebrews 4:13

41. See Matthew 4:3-10, 16:23; Luke 9:54-55

42. See John 18:10, 19

43. See Jude 8-11

44. Moore, Archie. "Law and Order Is The Only Edge We Have," *Republican Congressional Committee Newsletter,* April 15, 1968, p. 2.

45. Mark 14:62

46. John 19:10-11
47. I Peter 3:15
48. John 15:18-20, 16:33
49. See Revelation 13:17, 14:9-11
50. Matthew 27:28-29, 42
51. Luke 6:28
52. See James 3:10
53. Matthew 27:44
54. Luke 23:43
55. Isaiah 53:7
56. I Corinthians 5:12-13
57. John 14:17
58. Luke 23:34
59. See Isaiah 53:4-6
60. Philippians 8:10
61. Hebrews 10:36-39
62. Luke 22:34
63. 2 Corinthians 10:4
64. James 1:20
65. I Timothy 6:1
66. 2 Timothy 1:8
67. I Peter 2:19
68. Matthew 5:39
69. I Corinthians 15:56
70. Luke 23:34, 46
71. Isaiah 53:12
72. Philippians 4:11
73. Cavnar, *op. cit.*
74. I John 2:15
75. 2 Peter 2:20
76. James 1:27
77. James 4:4
78. I John 2:15
79. Matthew 24:37
80. Mark 13:31
81. Revelation 21:1
82. See I Corinthians 6:3, Revelation 20:10
83. See Matthew 25:32, Revelation 20:12

84. von Campenhausen, *op. cit.,* p. 156.

85. Matthew 5:14

86. Gordon, Paul. In a Bible study given in San Pedro, California, June 17, 1973.

87. Matthew 5:13

88. Private conversation with a member of "The Word of God," a charismatic Christian community in Ann Arbor, Michigan.

89. Private information.

90. Richter, Arthur. *Der Neue Mensch and Die Neue Gesellshaft,* pp. 53-54. R. Brockhaus Verlag, Wuppertal, 1973.

91. Schaeffer, Francis. *The Church at the End of the Twentieth Century,* pp. 50-52. The Norfolk Press, 19 Craycott Place, London S.W. 3, 1970.

92. Private information.

93. John 13:35

94. Synan, Vinson. *The Holiness Pentecostal Movement,* pp. 165ff. William B. Eerdmans Publishing Company, Grand Rapids, Michigan, 1971.

95. Mark 16:15

96. Acts 2:38

97. *The Commentator,* published by The American Lutheran Church, Office of the President.

98. Drummond, Henry. *Abstract Principles of Revealed Religion.* John Murray, London, 1845.

99. Strietelmeier, John. "Brother's Keeper or Sucker?" *Lutheran Standard,* April 11, 1961, p. 17.

100. Romans 14:23

101. Ephesians 5:5

102. Private information.

103. Private information.

104. Luke 16:19-31

105. Sayers, Dorothy. Quoted in *Journey To Easter* by Laurence Field, Augsburg Publishing House, Minneapolis, Minn., 1958, p. 17.

106. Erskin, John. "The Moral Obligation To Be Intelligent," *Fifty Great Essays* edited by Houston Peterson. Washington Square Press, Inc., New York, 1960, p. 330. (Address to Phi Beta Kappa Chapter, Amherst College, 1912.)

107. See James 2:15-17, I John 3:18

108. See Acts 6:2, Romans 10:14-15, I Corinthians 12:28, 2 Corinthians 5:16-18

109. Luke 12:22-23, 16:19-31, Matthew 6:19-21, 16:26

110. Luke 10:21

111. Luke 10:29

112. Isaiah 53:11

113. Hordern, William. In a lecture delivered at the Convention of the South Pacific District, The American Lutheran Church, Fresno, California, May 1970.

114. From promotional literature for "Project Neighbor," sponsored by The American Lutheran Church in 1970.

115. See Revelation 18:4

116. Galatians 6:10

117. Smith, Chuck. In private conversation.

118. John 13:35

119. Romans 11:14

120. Yamauchi, Edwin M. "How the Early Church Responded to Social Problems," Christianity Today, November 24, 1972, p. 186.

121. John 14:17

122. John 5:19

123. John 15:5

124. Philippians 2:8

125. I Corinthians 12:13

126. Hove, John. In private conversation.

127. Private information.

128. Private information.

129. Reported by The Bishop of Southwell at an International Charismatic Conference, Nottingham University, England, July 9, 1973.

130. Smails, Tom. In a lecture, July 9, 1973.

131. Richter, op. cit., pp. 59-60.

132. Hebrews 11:10

133. Prange, Erwin, op. cit., p. 144

134. Isaiah 9:6, Revelation 11:15

DA